BRISTOL OMNIBUS COMPANY

THE TWILIGHT YEARS

STEPHEN DOWLE

AMBERLEY

First published 2018

Amberley Publishing
The Hill, Stroud
Gloucestershire, GL5 4EP

www.amberley-books.com

ISBN 978 1 4456 7342 4 (print)
ISBN 978 1 4456 7343 1 (ebook)

British Library Cataloguing in Publication Data.
A catalogue record for this book is available from the British Library.

Typesetting by Amberley Publishing.
Printed in the UK.

Introduction

My connection with what was still in those days the Bristol Tramways & Carriage Co. must have begun while I was still a babe in arms. Neither of my parents ever learned to drive and the only means of reaching any destination beyond walking distance was the bus. In one of those insane misunderstandings of childhood, I conceived the idea that the upper deck had its own driver. This functionary's job, I imagined, was to precisely duplicate the movements of the man I'd seen in the cab below, so that the bus 'stayed together'. I thought that he sat somewhere behind and below the hatch at the front of the top deck, which, as I later discovered, actually gave access to the destination mechanism.

I found these early journeys by bus – usually to reach Bristol's new Broadmead shops – endlessly interesting. It would be difficult to explain exactly why. Perhaps it was because I could understand how the bus service worked by observing it in operation, rather as one can understand the functioning of a bicycle by looking at it. Aesthetic considerations came into it: everything from the Tilling Green, black mudguards and cream bands of the livery, to the tawny cigarette smoke patina of the upper deck ceiling and the pattern of the fabric on the seats brought satisfaction. I also liked the notices and their lettering, and the conductor's badges and items of equipment. Everything about buses pleased me.

One of the services we used, the 18, was provided from Eastville depot. Sometimes the bus stopped outside for a crew change. A ripple of groans passed among the passengers as, with a shudder, the engine was shut off and the driver lowered himself to the ground, causing the bus to rock slightly. The cab door slammed with a solid double snap. A few minutes with nothing to do are an agony of boredom to a child and I stared, with increasing restlessness, towards the depot's office, at whose threshold the fresh crew would eventually appear. Eastville was the home of the Leyland PD1s that had been added to the fleet in 1947–8. Already 'bus-aware', I had noticed the unfamiliar radiator and the different exhaust sound of these buses. Clearly I was well on the way to becoming a fully fledged enthusiast, or 'anorak', as such obsessives came to be known. The PD1s are about the earliest buses I clearly remember. More numerous were the K-types, and visits to an aunt at Pucklechurch meant a ride in an exotic five-cylinder L-type. The KSWs and LDs must have been around, but I didn't pay much attention to them until later, when, in approaching extinction, they assumed a tragic nobility.

By my early years in secondary school, in around 1961 or '62, I was a notebook-carrying 'bus spotter'. On Saturdays I haunted Bristol's bus station or, with a 5*s* half-fare 'Day Out' ticket, visited far-off parts of the company's area. The new FLF-type Lodekka became my great obsession. I had seen, in my Ian Allan *British Bus Fleets* book, that the first was numbered LC8540. I kept my eyes peeled, but never saw it. We had just returned from a family holiday in London and when out on my bicycle I now imagined myself an Underground train. One afternoon, braking smoothly to rest at the kerb (or platform, as I saw it) of Straits Parade, Fishponds, I found myself staring at the back of an FLF numbered LC7000. The number seemed to suggest 'first of type'. I memorised the registration number and, repeating it to myself, pedalled home as fast as I could. Ignoring my parents ('Where's your manners today, in your boots?') I stormed through the house and thudded up the stairs to consult my *British Bus Fleets*. Sure enough there it was, 995 EHW… the mystery was solved. Not long afterwards I experienced a 'shock of the new' when I saw one of the ex-Silver Star Leyland Atlanteans rumbling in through the bus station entrance, its hundreds of rivets catching the light from outside. I'd never seen anything like it. I aspired to ride on one of these fabulous vehicles at the earliest opportunity. This meant another Day Out ticket. I was filling notebooks like mad and had become an accomplished scholar of the company timetable.

This early schoolboy phase of my interest in buses had been succeeded by other preoccupations by the time I started working. My first job lasted for four years, but the firm moved to an impossibly distant site on the opposite side of Bristol and I needed another job quickly. It was well known that, because of its perennial staff shortage, almost anyone could walk into a job with the bus company; thus, having now exceeded the minimum age of eighteen, I applied to become a conductor. It was April 1970. I was put to work from Lawrence Hill depot on the 8/8A Warmley to Southmead service. It was an eye opener. The service (shortly afterwards renumbered 87/88) was, by common consent, the busiest in Bristol. Many journeys were not operated because crews could not be provided. Having 'one off in front' doubled the conductor's workload: five or six off in front led to scenes reminiscent of Dante's *Inferno*. Our passengers somehow saw platform staff as responsible for the poor service they suffered and were not inhibited from expressing their displeasure in terms of the most vindictive unpleasantness. This was quite illogical, as the crews, by being there and doing their jobs, reduced a problem that would otherwise be worse. I especially remember the respectable-looking thirtyish woman who, when I told my passengers that there was no driver to take the bus forward and that there would be a wait until I could transfer them onto the next bus, followed me out onto the pavement of St Augustine's Parade and, speaking in a slow, measured way, said, 'Why don't you go across the road and drown yourself in the harbour?' before spitting at me and walking off. This early 'conducting' phase of my time on the buses left me with a rather jaundiced view of human nature, which I've never quite shaken off. I've since had the utmost sympathy for any individual who is required to deal directly with the public in his or her work.

The job had started with a week at the Lawrence Hill training school. At the conclusion of the course ('Can I go over the Traffic Office and volunteer for overtime now?' asked one keen type) the instructor gave us a parting word of advice: 'There are two things you'll never get away with on this job ... drinking on duty and fiddling. Don't do either, you'll get caught'. I had led a sheltered life and didn't understand what was meant by 'fiddling'. Within hours of starting work on my first day I encountered passengers who invited me to 'keep the ticket'. The ticket machine was essentially a cash register and the ticket its receipt. No ticket meant no record of the transaction: the conductor could pocket the fare and the company was none the wiser. Travelling inspectors existed largely to deter this practice. I was so completely green and half-witted that I didn't even understand the etiquette of the matter, which was to keep half the fare and return half to the passenger, so that both parties benefited. I thought these passengers, in their charity, were simply trying to do me a favour. After about a fortnight I snapped out of it and from that point no passenger ever travelled on any bus of mine without a ticket for the full fare. When I encounter clueless behaviour by young people today I attempt, in imagination, to re-inhabit my younger self and recall how defective was my own understanding at their age.

Each week conductors moved one place up the duty roster and drivers one place down. This meant that you were paired with a particular driver for no more than a week at a time. I was sometimes glad of this. We were a fairly typical cross-section of working people, supplemented by occasional misfits, eccentrics, bankrupts, entrepreneurs riding out hard times, or professionals who'd had nervous breakdowns and been advised to take up a less stressful occupation – as, to outsiders, bus work must have seemed. The company's longest-serving employee during my early years was a driver called Nobby Clarke, who'd started as a points boy on the trams. Many of these old sweats had a fund of yarns going back to the days of petrol engines and solid tyres. Early every morning, it was told, in the days before self-starters, a five-man team went around the depot to start all the buses: one cranked the starting handle, two more assisted him by hauling on leather straps, another held a flaming rag to the air intake and the fifth sat in the cab to 'catch' the engine when it fired. This was a dangerous job: if the engine backfired the handle would whiplash backwards and break the forearms of the man doing the cranking. Eventually, a ratchet device was developed to prevent this. These older men, then nearing retirement, belonged to the generation that had been through the war and, although bus driving had been a reserved occupation, many had been in the forces. Theirs seemed more interesting characters, grounded in a larger experience; I preferred their company to that of my contemporaries, with their incessant chatter of pop music and football.

Not very long before, in 1963, the company had suffered opprobrium for operating a 'colour bar' in Bristol. This was unfair because the company was desperate to recruit staff from any source, and already employed 'coloured' labour in other parts of its area. The Bristol ban was insisted upon by the men's union. In those less politicised times, with the union operating a closed shop, it was not easy for the company to take a principled stand on the issue. By my time, recent immigrants made up a large proportion of the company's workforce. Those from India and Pakistan were not natural employees and tended to drift away, but while they lasted they brought an interesting element of 'diversity' to the job. Listening to a group of Pakistanis in the canteen was a free entertainment. From a torrent of rapid-fire Urdu the ears filtered out an occasional English phrase ('top of Park Street') or a term ('dogging', 'short dapper') from the company's elaborate internal lexicon. The West Indians gradually moved out from the inner city areas where they had first settled to mortgaged houses in the suburbs. They were easily assimilated into the life of the job. Soon they were participating in the exchange of garden produce that operated among staff and were a fixture of the perpetual canteen card schools. In my experience 'race relations' on the buses were a complete non-issue: in twenty years on the job, I don't recall a single instance of racially motivated unpleasantness.

An episode that remains distinct in my memory of these years is my walk-on part in the saga of the Marconi 'B-Line' bus location system. Four 'city' routes were selected for a trial. Barcoded metal plates, called 'beacons', were fixed to bus stop posts along each route. The city council had granted permission for lamp posts to be used. British Telecom were not so forthcoming with their telegraph poles; I think an application had to be separately submitted for each pole. The barcodes were read by a scanner mounted in the roof of the bus and its position was then transmitted to a control room in the company's building on the city centre. A driver and conductor had been taken off their normal duties to put up the beacons. When the conductor 'went sick', I was asked if I would care to take his place. Jobs like this tended to attract those who were drawn by the prospect of a 'cushy number', and, expecting a skive, I gladly accepted. We had an 'office' in a withdrawn LD Lodekka (No. L8297), which was parked in a corner of the Lawrence Hill yard. On the lower deck we stored the beacons; upstairs was a desk and a Bisley filing cabinet (how on earth had they got it up the stairs?), in which were kept records of all beacons so far deployed. We started at 04.00 so that we could get the beacons up before our van became an obstruction to traffic. By 08.30 we were back in our 'office' and passed the rest of the morning in marathon Ludo test match series. As an ex-country-fleet LD, our bus had platform doors, which we kept firmly closed. This impeded the approach of our boss if he came down on an errand from Berkeley House, giving valuable extra seconds in which to conceal our board, counters and dice. When tested, the Marconi system was found to work satisfactorily, but was never put to use. I never understood what good it did to know the whereabouts of the buses. What was the practical application of that knowledge? In theory, buses were to be fed into the service where long gaps developed, but they too were delayed in the traffic that had caused the gap.

'It's about time you went up the school, isn't it young man?' said Albert Bratchell, Lawrence Hill's District Traffic Superintendent, approaching me one morning in March 1976 as I paid in my takings. Mr Bratchell was a nice, mild-mannered busman of the old school, a type still numerous in the company's middle management. One-man operation (OMO) was, after a slow start, coming in fast, and the company was eager to train conductors as drivers; even complete non-drivers such as myself were eligible for a try-out. I found that this eagerness was not shared at the Employment Office: the man behind the desk pursed his lips and slowly shook his head when he asked what my previous driving experience was and I cheerfully answered: 'None.' On the first morning at the school the instructors took themselves off to one side to apportion the fresh intake among themselves; mutterings about 'another bloody novice' reached my ears. That first day was 'theory' and the second was spent in endless circuits of the depot yard going 'up and down the box', but on the third I clambered into the cab of an elderly KSW and drove for the first time on the public highway, from Aust roundabout, via Easter Compton, to Patchway. My first impression was that everything was in motion: the steering column shook violently from side to side, the gearstick quivered and all the fittings of the cab moved and rattled. By lunchtime my wristwatch had ceased to keep correct time and the next day, as I reached out to make a gearchange, the knob on the gearstick smashed its face. I now understood the reason for something I'd previously noticed only unconsciously – that bus drivers always used pocket watches, carried in the top pocket on a short chain from the lapel.

It was my induction into the mysteries of crash boxes, double de-clutching, snatch changes, clutch brakes, epicyclic brake bands and kindred matters. After three days the trainee took a preliminary test, at which obvious no-hopers were weeded out. I failed, but the examiner, Ernie Belcher, pronounced himself satisfied of my promise and allowed me to re-take the test after a further two days. With this hurdle behind me I went on to take the 'final'. The company's Chief Examiner, George Waters, luckily failed to notice that I rubbed the kerb in negotiating Crow Lane roundabout, Henbury. Back at the depot he produced a little flip-up book of road signs and seemed impressed when I unhesitatingly identified countdown markers to a concealed level crossing. Perhaps it was to this alone that I owed my pass certificate and PSV licence. After a further two days of RE tuition I found myself driving out of Lawrence Hill depot in an FLF Lodekka (No. 7182) to pick up my first passengers. These were two charwomen, who boarded outside the Wayfarers pub in Charlton Road, Southmead, happily ignorant that I was driving in an official capacity for the first time, in a type of vehicle of which my total experience amounted to two circuits of the depot yard the previous afternoon. I later came to doubt the wisdom of allowing complete novice drivers to take the controls of a bus carrying seventy or eighty people after no more than a fortnight's tuition. It took me six months to feel confident, but I soon bought a pocket watch, proudly carried on its chain in my top pocket.

'They sends 'em down 'ere,' grumbled Charlie Stevens, the Marlborough Street duty clerk, rolling his eyes to the ceiling as he addressed Senior Inspector Bert 'Polly' Flinders, 'and they ain't OMO-trained or National-trained.' He sat back in his chair and, to indicate his suffering, tossed his company-issue indelible pencil into the disordered paperwork on his desk. Standing on the opposite side of the desk I shifted uncomfortably in my uniform. I was due to transfer to Marlborough Street depot the next Monday and had come to make myself known and enquire which duty I was to start on. I had qualified as a driver just as the last rear-entrance and the first forward-entrance buses were being withdrawn. In my early months I notched up a few LDs, a single FS and a handful of FSFs. After that the 87/88s were worked by FLFs and – following disturbances on late-night buses – by crewed, radio-equipped REs in the evenings. When I'd been driving about a year, I was waiting one afternoon at the city centre to 'take on' at the start of a late turn. To my surprise the bus that turned up was an MW, No. 2560. Assenting to the derogatory opinions of my conductor, but secretly pleased, I shimmied into position behind the wheel and we chugged off into the traffic. The enjoyable few hours that followed increased the slight dissatisfaction I'd felt at driving only two types of bus at Lawrence Hill. After a short period of vacillation I applied for a transfer to Bristol's bus station, where there was a more varied fleet. As a depot, the bus station was known as Marlborough Street.

Hence the exasperation of Charlie Stevens. It was 'union agreement' that any driver transferring to a new depot had to start on a crew roster. The Marlborough Street staff demographic was rather older than at other depots. Its two remaining 'crew' routes (Bath and Thornbury) were staffed by long-service men disinclined to adapt to OMO: in practice there were only OMO vacancies at the depot. There was Marlborough Street crying out for OMO drivers, lamented Charlie, and they goes and sends him another bloody crew bloke… me! Not only was I not OMO-trained, but I hadn't been familiarised with Leyland Nationals either. Knowing that it was a waste of breath, I pointed out that I'd been a conductor for six years and there was really no need for the OMO training, but this cut no ice – procedures were in place. In the end Charlie killed two birds with one stone and I was OMO-trained on a Leyland National as a couple of hours' overtime. After a statutory fortnight on the crew roster, I found myself a fully fledged OMO driver. The city services were still worked entirely by six-day-week rosters. Marlborough Street had adopted five-day working, but retained two six-day rosters. I put in for one of these – the 'OMO 4' roster – knowing that it covered most of the lesser services typically worked by the fast-disappearing MWs. Here, for the first time, I was able to ease Charlie's difficulties: because it was 'six-day' and handled a lot of the unpopular MW work, the roster was difficult to keep fully staffed.

'D'you know the Radstocks?' asked the depot foreman one morning, not long after my transfer. He was referring to the web of routes linking Bristol with the former colliery towns of North Somerset.

'No,' I answered.

'Well here's your chance to learn,' he replied grimly and, I thought, with a hint of relish. The foreman, then a few years from retirement, was a Senior Inspector, former wartime sergeant and member of the Burma Star Association. I was a new boy, in my mid-twenties but looking considerably younger, who had lately transferred from a 'city' depot. To such a man I must have represented a new generation of young whippersnappers who didn't know what the job was 'all about'. I was the Marlborough Street 04.30 Spare, whose function was to stand by in case any driver went sick, overslept or otherwise failed to turn up. I had never been to Radstock, had only a vague notion of where it was and knew little of the geography of North Somerset, on the opposite side of Bristol from my native regions. It was now six o'clock on a filthy winter's morning and the scratchy sound against the windowpanes told me that rain was lashing down in the empty streets outside. At Whitchurch, Bristol's street lighting receded in the wing mirrors and I was in pitch blackness. The wipers reciprocated sluggishly across the windscreen with a monotonous whirring sound. Knowing that it would make no difference, I switched on the MW's demisters – in practice, you used your sleeve. The tiny mirrors, partially eclipsed on the nearside by the upper part of the folding entrance door, were fogged up and flecked with mud drawn up in the bus's slipstream. It was all seat-of-the-pants stuff. I hadn't a clue where I was supposed to be going and had not yet picked up any passenger from whom I could ask directions. In any case, I hated doing this; I felt such a damned fool. Several times I shot past turnings and had to reverse. I missed a peak-hour deviation in Paulton and abandoned the attempt to do a school run, being unable to discover the point from which it started. Subsequently, there was a telephoned complaint from the headmaster. It was an inglorious occasion.

Yet, in time, the Radstocks became favourites of mine and typified the kind of work I enjoyed. I was not fond of services such as those to Bath or Weston-super-Mare, which essentially kept to a charmless main road: I liked a *permutated* route, with plenty of peak-hour deviations, school variants and short journeys, preferably deep in the country, far from dual-carriageways, street lighting and roundabouts. Doynton (Church), Didmarton (King's Arms), East Harptree (Clock), Chew Magna (Post Office), Stanton Drew (Roundhouse), Ubley (Saw Mills) and even Cadbury Heath (Co-op)... there was poetry in these things. Eternity is in love with the compilers of the amended timetables – as William Blake may not have said. Although I moaned about the job like everyone else, in looking back from the viewpoint of the modern workplace those years seem a golden age of humane employment and enlightened paternalism. If you could tolerate the early starts and the split turns there were far worse ways of earning a living. The memory screens out the less enjoyable aspects of the job and today I see myself pottering along sun-dappled lanes, drawing into market towns of honeyed stone, or bowling across broad hilltops with the gleaming brown waters of the Severn and the Welsh hills spread out before me. It has been my experience that pleasant, congenial work never lasts.

The industry's fortunes had been going from bad to worse for twenty years. In 1980 the Market Analysis Project (MAP) was established to identify which were the profitable and which the loss-making parts of the network. Subsequently, the company espoused a policy of merging its main services with the few revenue-generating parts of the remainder, while completely abandoning what was unprofitable. This meant carrying more passengers on fewer vehicles operating less mileage. The ground was being prepared for legislation that led, in 1986, to the deregulation and privatisation of the industry. Some years earlier, in 1978, the Joint Services agreement between the company and Bristol City Council had been ended after forty-two years. Though I do not know for certain, it seems plausible that the ending of this anomalous arrangement was also part of a long-term strategy to prepare the company for sale. These were the twilight years. The company was broken up into a number of 'operating units' and disposed of in a series of management buyouts. The parts eventually vanished into new bus-operating syndicates. Thus, the Bristol Omnibus Company, uniquely distinguished among provincial bus operators, tiptoed without ceremony from the national transport scene. It was very much a case of 'not with a bang, but a whimper'. I left the part of the company that had become Badgerline in 1990.

The photographs in the book were taken between 1975 and 1980, during those declining years of the company's existence. I have included some shots illustrating the 'works' fleet. The ancillary fleets of bus operators are a neglected aspect of omnibological studies and many of the vehicles, being confined to depots and works, went unseen by outsiders. I have also taken the liberty of including a few photographs of ex-company vehicles that were to be seen at the time with subsequent owners. Although the photographs tend to go from earlier to later, no strict chronological order or other form of arrangement has been attempted.

As more modern buses languished in their depots due to a famine of spare parts and the company awaited delivery of new vehicles, the KSWs found themselves pressed into an active old age. The last examples were allocated to Muller Road, which also 'fed' Staple Hill depot. Accordingly Gloucester Road and Fishponds Road became the final haunts of the type. No. C8429 (YHT 924), new in 1957, still had eight months to go when photographed climbing out of the city, bound for Blackhorse, on Tuesday 28 October 1975.

Newly delivered LHs are seen at Lawrence Hill during the evening of Monday 5 January 1976. None had yet received a destination blind (a 'linen', in company parlance) or fleet number. In February KHU 324P entered service at Marlborough Street depot as No. 374. The LH was a basic vehicle that was said to have been intended for a working life of only seven years. In the event, few of Bristol's attained even that age, being prematurely withdrawn after the large-scale abandonment of rural services that followed the Market Analysis Project (MAP). Many went on to further service far from their original home.

My only photograph of a bus in the company's agreeable OMO livery, which was intended to identify all one-man-operated vehicles to their passengers – although I doubt whether it made them any more attentive to the matter of having their fares ready. The livery had been killed off by the standard 'leaf green' of the National Bus Company (NBC) and was almost extinct in the active fleet by this time. No. 2957 (977 DAE), an MW5G dating from 1959, was photographed at Lawrence Hill depot on Wednesday 26 March 1975. It had been withdrawn ('delicensed', to use the company term) the previous September, but wasn't disposed of until June.

Following the opening of the M32 in 1975, the company introduced a peak-hour, limited-stop service, numbered 62, between the city centre and the suburb of Bromley Heath. FLF No. 7054 (222 NAE) belonged to the 'country' fleet and had probably been allocated to this duty for its five-speed gearbox. It is seen working the evening outward journey on Monday 5 April 1976.

The company was late to accept the VRT and didn't receive large numbers until after ECW had re-designed the bodywork with the 'BET' curved windscreen. The eight K-registered examples with the earlier flat-fronted style were, therefore, always distinctive. They had been the first one-man double-deckers in Bristol and were used to convert the 22/23 service in 1972. Complications arose because there were not enough of the new buses to provide the entire service and the shortage had to be made up with single-deck REs. Who was paid double or single-deck rate, when and on what vehicles, resulted in a pay scale of labyrinthine complexity. No. C5006 (EHU 365K) is seen on Redcliffe Hill on Wednesday 7 April 1976 while operating the long-established 21 service.

The lads in the paint shop – just over my right shoulder as I took this shot – must have been chuffed with this outstanding example of their craft, advertising a Clifton travel agency. All-over advertising liveries had first appeared in 1971 and were, in my view, a deplorable development. RELL No. C1240 (AHU 734J), new in June 1971, had received its fancy paint job in October 1975.

Bristol AVW-engined LD No. LC8479 (819 CHU) had been placed in service at Eastville depot in 1958. Following its withdrawal in October 1973, it was appropriated by the Central Repair Works (CRW) and disappeared indoors for the company's engineering apprentices to practice on, becoming training bus No. W149. It is seen here in January 1976, making a rare appearance out of doors and still carrying the pre-NBC Bristol Joint Services livery and fleet name. The neighbouring FLF (No. C7306) had suffered a collision that morning while operating one of the services to Brislington School.

In about 1976, the 87 service (historically the 8A) was re-routed to terminate at Filton (instead of Arnside Road, Southmead), with alternate journeys extended to the new Bristol Polytechnic building in Coldharbour Lane. This added a round trip of about 3 miles to the route and, in order to slot the vehicles in with the rest of the service, an overlay of about half an hour was necessary. This was popular with crews, who were granted the use of the college refectory, with its coffee machine and other amenities. Seen on Friday 18 February 1977, Bristol-engined FLF No. C7108 (801 SHW) waits at the bleak Polytechnic terminus, with its freshly laid turf and the mud of recent construction.

In October 1978 Bristol loaned three 11.3-metre Leyland Nationals from Marlborough Street depot to Midland Red. On Saturday 17 February 1979, your intrepid photographer tracked down two of them on the town services in Tamworth. It is believed the third went to Cannock. As a driver at Marlborough Street I had often driven these buses, and it was with a slight sense of dislocation in time and space that I encountered them in these alien surroundings. No. 3035 (NFB 603R) and its fellows were returned to Bristol the following July.

In 1967 the company stepped into the breach when neighbouring Western National wanted to order twenty FSF Lodekkas: Bristol Commercial Vehicles had inconveniently discontinued the model some years earlier. Bristol parted with twenty of its thirty-eight examples. In 1970 the NBC handed over Western National's Trowbridge enclave to Bristol Omnibus Co. and Western National ungratefully reallocated several elderly and otherwise unwanted vehicles to Trowbridge so that they could be dumped on the Bristol company, including several of the FSFs. Thus, No. 6031 (728 JHY) came back to see out its final years with its original owner.

It was always interesting to encounter company vehicles with subsequent owners. This Gardner-engined K-type had been new in 1948 as Bristol Tramways No. 3741 (LAE 316). Its body was rebuilt by ECW in 1957 and it was withdrawn in October 1965. Brain's Food Products ran a fleet of staff buses from its factory in Bridge Road, Lower Soundwell. Although they were acquired through a dealer and might have come from any previous owner, only ex-Bristol vehicles were purchased. They were familiar throughout Bristol's easterly suburbs.

KSW No. C8373 (WHW 814) is seen shortly after leaving Hanham depot on the afternoon of Thursday 24 July 1975, probably to pick up service from Kingswood on the 97 route. This was a morning and evening round-the-houses affair mainly laid on for schools. In October the bus was withdrawn after being lightly damaged in a freak accident. It skidded on a patch of paint that had been spilled by workmen who were applying a fresh coat to the railings in the middle of the Haymarket. The bus crashed through the railings, crossed the opposite carriageway and pirouetted to a halt on the pavement outside Lewis's department store, facing the way it had come.

Ground zero for the city service dual-door REs during the late seventies was the east side of Colston Avenue, where buses on the 7/8 service jostled for kerb space with other RE-operated routes. The 7/8 was a hectic little service – city centre conditions made time-keeping difficult and on Bank Holidays it was sometimes duplicated with double-deckers to cope with zoo traffic. Here, on Monday 14 January 1980, a full complement of passengers glumly wait for a fresh driver aboard No. 1246 (BHY 702J), as others loiter on the pavement weighing up the options: to await the by no means assured arrival of a driver and save themselves a stiff walk up Park Street, or leg it and save 10p… with the bus probably passing them midway between stops.

As well as their passenger-carrying fleets, all large bus companies operated considerable numbers of auxiliary vehicles, often of considerable interest. Recovery wagons and driver-training buses were the most familiar to the public, but No. W140 (VJB 283) was a Karrier ES341 lorry with hydraulic platform. The 'W' prefix stood for 'works' fleet. The company acquired it in July 1972. It was probably used for such tasks as maintaining floodlights and other overhead equipment in sheds and yards.

No. C1401 (JHU 842L), an early 11.3-metre Leyland National with dual doors, waits under the 'Cheltenham Road arches' at the starting point of the circuitous 83 service on Saturday 19 February 1977. The passengers must wait a few moments for the driver to enter the machine readings on his 'waybill' – a term of considerable antiquity, to be found in descriptions of stagecoach travel in the writings of Dickens and Surtees. The National was imposed, more or less compulsorily, on the subsidiaries of the NBC; for ex-Tilling companies like Bristol it represented a departure from previous buying policy.

In 1973 the company acquired five Plaxton-bodied Leyland Leopard PSU3/3RT coaches that had been new to Southdown in 1966. Some were used with two-man crews on peak-hour extras in Bristol, still carrying Southdown livery. They were soon repainted into National coach colours and saw another five years' service. No. 2172 (EUF 213D) was found in Kensington depot, Bath, on Saturday 21 February 1976. Southdown's original batch was broken up and distributed among various NBC subsidiaries and Bristol's five examples were not consecutively registered.

A scene inside the CRW paint shop, Lawrence Hill, taken on Tuesday 2 March 1976. FLF No. C7151 (844 SHW) was being painted back into fleet livery after spending the previous two and a half years as an all-over advertisement for Haskins Furniture. Alongside, RELL No. G1270, from the Gloucester city fleet, was receiving a fresh coat. The date of a vehicle's last repaint was usually to be found marked up inside the cab. All painting was done by hand; masking would have taken too long and been too expensive in labour.

There was a time when all you had to do to see interesting buses was look out of the window. Drifting past my bedroom on Friday 21 November 1975 was this rather rare bird: excluding open-toppers at Weston-super-Mare, No. 8550 (440 FHW) was one of only four FS Lodekkas in the Bristol fleet. Until a few months before, it had always been at Swindon, but was now seeing out its last days at Lawrence Hill, probably in connection with 'mileage balancing'. The 380 service was operated by Hanham depot, which, only being equipped for routine servicing, was supplied with vehicles from Lawrence Hill.

Some FLF Lodekkas saw almost twenty years of service, but this one only just made it to twelve. The problem was, I think, that supplies of Bristol engine spares became increasingly uncertain. The company re-engined some of its last Bristol-engined FLFs with Gardner engines to ensure a supply of spares into their old age. Thereafter, Bristol-engined examples, such as No. C7208 (DHW 988C), tended to fall by the wayside. The bus is seen, on Thursday 26 January 1978, during a brief second career as a temporary Allocator's Office. The approaching figure is Sheila, making her way home after a shift serving toast, sausage cobs and cups of weak, over-milked tea in the staff canteen.

From an engineering point of view, rear engines are far from ideal. Cooling is always problematical and remoteness from the driver doesn't help. Several REs went up in flames during the early days of the type, and BOC was not alone in suffering from the problem. It was unfortunate that No. C1138 (UHY 633H) should have suffered an engine fire after receiving an all-over advertising livery publicising the company's concessionary fares. It was photographed at Lawrence Hill on Thursday 6 May 1978. It was repaired and returned to service and another RE was used to advertise Fare Cards.

As one of six 'stretched' LDs built for various companies in 1957, when legislation first permitted 30-foot double-deckers, the company's single LDL was definitely a collector's item. The model never went into production, the 30-foot rear-entrance Lodekka becoming the FL, which was itself destined to remain an uncommon type. After several unsuccessful attempts to photograph the bus – No. L8450 (YHT 962) – I tracked it down on Monday 22 December 1975 at Kensington depot, Bath, after it had been withdrawn. But look where they parked it! I'd presciently brought a wide-angle lens, which enabled me to get this less-than-ideal shot. Note the extra emergency exit behind the cab, and that someone had taken the registration plate as a trophy.

The final KSWs gravitated to Muller Road depot and spent much of their time on the gruelling services up and down the congested Gloucester Road. No. C8427 (YHT 923), new in 1957, is seen during its final days on Wednesday 3 December 1975. It was withdrawn because of a defect, officially on the 31st. Withdrawals always occurred on the last day of the month, presumably because the company wished to get maximum use before surrendering licences, tax discs etc. Identification of Gardner-engined KSWs was always easy because of the two apertures in the engine side panel, for access to the oil filler caps, corresponding to the two blocks of three cylinders.

It was to the film *Ice Cold in Alex* that my thoughts turned whenever I saw this vehicle from the 'works' fleet. No. W29 was a Ford Canada gun tractor, ex-Ministry of Supply and presumably of Second World War vintage. One imagines the crew, four each side, sitting under a canvas canopy, each with a fag in the corner of his mouth – Players, from the NAAFI – screwing up his eyes against the smoke and grumbling. The platoon commander sits up front with the driver, Corporal Bennett. 'Petrol' is lettered on the fuel tank. The company's address, once one of the most familiar in the city, is still given as 1–3 St Augustine's Place.

Withdrawn MWs, each with a 'Delicensed' sticker in its nearside windscreen, are lined up at Bath awaiting disposal to dealers on Saturday 21 February 1976. For a relatively small bus, the MW was remarkably heavy and ponderous. They were not well liked by drivers, among whom they were disparagingly known as 'conker-boxes'. They had bags of character though: the correct strategy was simply to accept that they wouldn't do anything quickly and adapt your technique accordingly.

On Friday 2 April 1976, KSW No. C8374 (WHW 815) is driven into Staple Hill depot by a fitter after being taken out of service as defective. The passengers must already have continued to Blackhorse aboard a replacement, and the next bus, provided by LD No. C8505 (830 CHU), for New Cheltenham, has caught up. The company continued to buy the KSW, which was cheaper, for as long as it remained available, the LD being ordered only where it was needed for routes with low bridges. Final withdrawals of the two types occurred only a few months apart. Both buses were in their final weeks and No. C8374 became the last KSW in service.

In 1961 the company took delivery of a small batch of FS convertibles for the open-top seafront service at Weston-super-Mare. The pleasing livery, so reminiscent of ice cream, was wholly appropriate to a seaside resort. No. 8576 (866 NHT), with its roof fitted for the coming winter, was photographed on Friday 7 November 1975. For the next season the open-toppers were repainted in garish pictorial liveries and given names.

Seen newly delivered on an earlier page, LH No. 374 (KHU 324P) had, by Tuesday 12 July 1977, completed eighteen months' service operating from Bristol's Marlborough Street depot. The photograph must have been taken at around 06.30: the bus, having travelled out from Bristol to Olveston (Post Office), would now depart at 06.38 for Filton – one of many journeys laid on for workers at the Rolls-Royce and BAC aircraft factories. It would return and, after a second dodgy reversal at the side of St Mary's Church, leave at 07.46 with the morning's 'office wallahs' for Bristol.

On Saturday 23 October 1976, RELL No. 1279 (EHU 380K) reaches one of the extremities of the Bristol company's system. The bus, new in May 1972, prepares to work back to its Trowbridge base as poppy red Leyland Nationals of the Hants & Dorset fleet jostle for platform space at Salisbury's bus station.

In 1977 the company acquired five LHs that had been new to Thames Valley and were withdrawn by its successor, Alder Valley, when they became due for recertification overhauls. No. 346 (VMO 227H) was the oldest and dated from 1969. It was a notable crate. Having gone to the expense of re-certifying the buses, the company got only around two years' service from them and could not have known that soon, in the wake of MAP, it would be trying to dispose of its own LHs when only eighteen months old. This bus was withdrawn a couple of weeks after being re-wired and given new seats. It is seen on Saturday 9 September 1978 on the A38 at Almondsbury.

Seen in the yard of Lawrence Hill depot on Friday 16 May 1975, LS No. 3000 (PHW 934) had entered service, as No. 2844, in 1954. It was first withdrawn in 1967. After several reinstatements, its five-cylinder engine was replaced by a six-cylinder unit and it was internally refurbished to the standard of current REs, re-entering service in February 1971. This was intended as the beginning of a large-scale refurbishment of the LS-type, but the government's bus grant scheme, which paid half the cost of a new vehicle, made the scheme uneconomic and it was abandoned when just eight buses had been upgraded. No. 3000 lasted until March 1976.

Acquired by the company in 1970 as part of the transfer of Western National's Trowbridge area – and none too welcome I imagine – was this lowbridge-bodied, Bristol AVW-engined KSW, new in December 1951. Not long after the change of ownership it was damaged in an accident but, rather surprisingly, was repaired and reinstated as a training vehicle. Just visible is the four-abreast upper-deck seating with offside sunken gangway. No. W139 (LTA 843) is seen at Lawrence Hill on Saturday 4 March 1978. It was withdrawn shortly afterwards and passed into preservation, but was vandalised and scrapped.

The strains of what sounded like Mantovani and His Orchestra mellifluated into the street from speakers on the pavement. The former No. 7023 (818 MHW), a Bristol-engined FLF dating from 1961, had been withdrawn at the end of February 1977. By June it had passed to Bose Hi-Fi of Sittingbourne as a mobile showroom. On Wednesday 2 November 1977 it had returned to its native place and was found promoting its owner's wares in Bristol's Broadmead shopping centre. I exchanged a few words with the custodian, who lamented the tedium of driving the bus all the way down the M4 at its top speed of 45 mph.

With the debauch of Christmas well over and spring still a long way off, six-cylinder MW No. 2433 (BHU 97C) approaches Stroud's bus station on the afternoon of Saturday 8 January 1977, during the one month of the year of which there is nothing favourable to be said. The bus had entered service in the Bristol Greyhound coach fleet as No. 2143 in April 1965. It was downgraded to dual-purpose status in February 1971, withdrawn at the end of January 1979 and briefly loaned to South Wales Transport.

At eighteen years old, KSW No. C8427 (YHT 923) was still earning its keep on one of Bristol's bread-and-butter services, the 74 to Patchway. It was uphill all the way, in and out of the parked cars and lorries making deliveries from their tail-lifts, stopping at every fourth lamp post. It is seen on Tuesday 5 August 1975 in Lewins Mead, a minute or two after commencing its journey from the city centre. Bringing up the rear is one of its Muller Road stablemates, VRT No. C5024 (MHW 291L), which, when new, had probably replaced an earlier KSW.

The city services had once operated on a cross-city basis, but a change of policy during the early seventies led to most being terminated in the central area. The 73/74 replaced the various routes that served the main A38 Gloucester Road out of the city. When photographed in Colston Avenue on Tuesday 30 December 1975, LD6G No. C8457 (YHT 944) had precisely six months to go, being withdrawn on the last day of June 1976.

Although it had slyly returned several of the FSFs acquired from Bristol in 1967 by re-allocating them just before Bristol took over Trowbridge depot, the remainder continued to serve the fickle Western National company. On Thursday 19 February 1976 this pair was found at Taunton bus station. 701 and 704 JHY had entered service as Nos GL8562 (of the Gloucester city fleet) and L8565, before Bristol adopted 60XX and 70XX fleet numbers for its forward-entrance Lodekkas. The 27-foot 6-inch forward-entrance FSF found few takers, operators preferring the higher seating capacity of the 30-foot FLF.

The Barnsley trade plate (628 HE) carried by the towing lorry leaves us in no doubt that the next and final stop for Bristol-engined FLF No. C7088 (531 OHU) will be one of the breakers' yards at Carlton. The company usually removed advertising and marks of ownership before disposing of buses, but this had not been done, probably because the vehicle's withdrawal had been hastened by an engine defect and there was no likelihood of its being sold on. The photograph was taken on Saturday 26 February 1977 outside the Traffic Office at Lawrence Hill. The tow truck driver was probably making a last-minute visit to the staff toilets – it was a long way to Yorkshire.

The first of the RESLs was No. 500 (THU 346G). With the same 11.1 litre Leyland 0.680 engine that was fitted to their longer brethren they were notably lively performers, though more than seemed explicable by a little less weight and fewer seats; possibly the impression was 'psychological', in that they were more manoeuvrable and easier to 'throw around'. They had short lives and disappeared en masse in the great cull of smaller buses that started at the end of the seventies. The bus is seen at Swindon bus station on Saturday 14 January 1978. It was withdrawn in September the following year. The company scrapped it for body parts at Lawrence Hill.

I had just bought a wide-angle lens and was getting 'creative' on this shot, taken Monday 28 April 1975 as I passed through Fishponds on the top deck of an FLF – probably heading for home after a spree among Bristol's record and book shops. Heading into the city was No. C8431 (YHT 927), Bristol's last KSW and also the last built. New in October 1957, it was in the last four months of service in Bristol, but was afterwards exported for further use in Macau, where it was modified with an extra door at the front and full-depth sliding windows.

Withdrawn MW5Gs parked at the side of Wells bus station on Friday 8 October 1976: the former No. 2517 (352 MHU) and No. 2505 (527 JHU) had both been taken out of traffic on 30 June. As was customary the blinds had been salvaged, tax discs and licenses removed and there are no fleet numbers. As time went on few MWs reached the end of their days still carrying their Bristol-ECW badges and formalised 'wings', which were coveted trophies.

In March 1973, nicely in time for that year's summer season, the company acquired a pair of Bristol-engined LD convertibles for the Weston-super-Mare seafront service. To the trained observer it was all in the Chester registration number: No. 8581 (627 HFM) had come from Crosville Motor Services and must have been a veteran of the North Wales coastal resorts. It is seen outside Weston's town hall on Friday 7 November 1975. It is thought the company re-engined the bus with a Gardner LW. At the time of writing it survives on private hire work in the north of England and is super-powered by a Gardner LX engine.

This photograph, taken on the smashing autumn morning of Monday 23 October 1978, could not be repeated today. The bus, of course, is long gone, but so too is the setting. If the ground had opened up the bus would have dropped straight into the Severn Tunnel, whose 'English' portal was in a cutting off right of this view. Running along the right-hand side of the road was the track bed of the little railway line that once connected the Severn Beach branch to the South Wales main line at Pilning. All this was obliterated when the second Severn Bridge was constructed. The bus, RELL No. 1208 (YHY 588J), was working the 08.00 journey from Bristol on the 324 service to Severn Beach.

The 77/78 service was historically the 7/7A. The renumbering of this and several other routes had come to pass in a minor revamp of services in August 1970. The current General Manager decreed that each route should have a unique number. It seemed to me an unnecessary solution to a non-problem and I disliked the way it seemed to reduce the 'seniority' of the lowest-numbered services which, although they changed over the years, had originated as tram-replacement routes. Along with all the other Bristol-engined FSFs, No. C6029 (725 JHY) was to be withdrawn on 30 June 1976. It is pictured, Henbury-bound, in Filton Road, Horfield, on Wednesday 3 December 1975.

In 1969, the company donated all but four of the Gardner-engined FLFs in the 'city' fleet to West Riding Autos. The Wakefield-based company had participated in development of the advanced Guy Wulfrunian double-decker and had bought almost all that were produced. Unfortunately, they proved unreliable and were rapidly withdrawn when West Riding became part of the NBC. By the time this photograph was taken the crisis was long over and the ex-Bristol vehicles were surplus to requirements. Those still in service were passed to the Lincolnshire Road Car Co. Still carrying West Riding's red livery, but with LINCOLNSHIRE fleet names, the former Bristol No. C7290 (JAE 630D) is seen in Scunthorpe on Wednesday 9 October 1978.

The dual-purpose, or 'semi-coach', RELH was intended to operate longer distance 'stage carriage' bus services but might, during the summer, find itself pressed into service as part of the company's contribution to the National Express coach pool – although this was discouraged by NBC management. In practice ('There's a posh bus we've got today, driver.') it could crop up anywhere. I found them too high-geared for ordinary bus work. It was seldom possible to utilise their extra turn of speed and you tended to creep ahead of schedule if you did. Bath's No. 2065 (WHW 377H) is seen reposing at its home depot on Saturday 21 February 1976.

With FLFs now being withdrawn from the main fleet, No. L8537 (989 EHW) must have been one of the last LDs to be converted to a driver trainer. On Thursday 2 September 1976 the job was almost finished and only a trip across the yard to the paint shop was lacking. The bus passed into the training fleet as No. W162. The FLF in the distance with its engine cowl removed was, I think, No. C7060, which had been withdrawn at the end of June, reportedly due to an 'engine defect'. There was a hole about the size of a saucer in the side of the engine, corresponding to the position of the fifth cylinder.

For fun I loved the FLFs and MWs, but for doing the job the RE was, in my opinion, never bettered. Unlike the swimmy Leyland National, it had a confidence-boosting solidity and sure-footedness; its semi-automatic transmission ideally combined control with ease. It had the best brakes of any bus. If it had a vice – and nothing in life is perfect – it was the atrocious rattling of the Plexiglass screen behind the driving seat. Posed in Castle Road, Walton St Mary, on Monday 19 June 1978, No. 1041 (MHW 850F) is seen operating the 10.01 journey from Bristol on the half-hourly service to Clevedon.

As any former conductor will confirm, there is no colder place than the interior of a bus at four o'clock in the morning after it has been standing for four or five hours on a winter's night. Buses with open rear platforms were that much worse. I have myself demonstrated that it was possible to scrape frost from the inside of the windows using the edge of a clipboard. Awaiting the stab of the driver's thumb on their starter buttons the next morning was this line-up of FLF Lodekkas, seen at Lawrence Hill on the night of Tuesday 18 November 1975.

Bristol-engined KSW No. C8108 (OHY 965) was converted to a tree-lopper after a collision with a low bridge in April 1966, becoming No. W120. Not a few buses suffered such accidents as a result of drivers taking unauthorised routes when running 'off service'. The railway bridges in Gipsy Patch Lane or St Luke's Road were the usual culprits. The purpose of this vehicle was to prevent damage to double-deckers by cutting back overhanging branches. The Ford Transit van on the right probably belonged to the bill posters – the functionaries who attended to timetable displays at bus stops and kindred matters.

These were the days when you didn't feel ashamed to pick up your wage packet at the end of the week – leaving aside that we may already have been 'monthly by BACS' by the time of this photograph. The 14.32 journey on the 370 service to Cheddar had not operated the previous day, the whole route being impassable, but mild airs fresh from the balmy Atlantic had set in, and on Tuesday 21 February 1978 the snow was melting fast. Wrington and Langford were still cut off, but all parts of the route that could be reached were to be served. However, no passengers used the service so dutifully provided. MW5G No. 2605 (BHY 712C), new in 1965, was withdrawn later in the year.

With only three months to go, FLF No. 7105 (550 OHU) gets going from Swindon bus station on Saturday 14 January 1978 with the 12.45 departure for Highworth on service 473. The bus was a minor oddity in that it had acquired the early style of Lodekka front grille, perhaps in an accident repair. It went on to serve with that great accumulator of second-hand Lodekkas, Top Deck Travel. Although the LD was preferred, the company placed great trust in the ruggedness and reliability of these vehicles by operating them on overland tours to the Middle East and Asia.

A happy pairing of two ex-Gloucester vehicles, snapped just inside the London Road entrance of Bath's Kensington depot on Tuesday 21 September 1976. The FSF, No. 6039 (804 MHW), had started life in the Gloucester city fleet in November 1961 and had been transferred to the 'country' fleet, shedding the distinction of a 'G'-prefix fleet number, in January 1971. It was withdrawn nine days after the photograph was taken. RELL No. 1096 (RHT 145G), new in December 1968, had been transferred to Bath as recently as the previous June. This is now the car park of a Morrisons supermarket.

Production of the LD Lodekka straddled the changeover from the Bristol AVW engine to the less well-regarded BVW. No. 8569 (982 EHW), new in August 1959 as No. L98 in the Cheltenham District Traction fleet, was fitted with the BVW. When photographed at the town's Royal Well bus station on Tuesday 6 January 1976, it still bore the CHELTENHAM fleet name, though by this time the sub-fleet had lost its red livery. Later deliveries of LDs were equipped with the Cave-Brown-Cave engine-cooling and saloon-heating apparatus, whose air intakes can be seen on either side of the destination screen. The bus had three months left, being withdrawn at the end of April.

A pair of withdrawn LDs, each with its 'Delicensed' sticker, awaits disposal at Kensington depot, Bath, on Saturday 21 February 1976. The conductor, emerging from the Traffic Office, removes his uniform tunic and slings it over his shoulder: it was a glorious sunny day, with spring coming on. No. 8401 (WHY 954), on the left, was Gardner-powered, but No. 8432 (YHT 948) had a Bristol AVW engine. White steering wheels were introduced, at a time when older buses were 7 feet 6 inches wide, as a reminder to the driver that he was in control of an 8-footer.

Throughout the sixties and early seventies the company was handicapped by an appalling shortage of staff. Crewless buses taken out of service at relief points around the city centre were taken to Canon's Marsh to avoid obstructing traffic. Long ranks of unmanned vehicles formed during most days and the public endured an extremely poor service. By the later 1970s, service reductions and higher unemployment had reduced the problem. Occasional minor shortages continued to occur and on Saturday 26 May 1979 a line-up of five unmanned buses, led by VRT No. 5074 (MOU 748R), stands in the shadow of one of the city's towering tobacco bonds, which has now vanished.

No. C1456 (NWS 903R) was an 11.3-metre, dual-door Leyland National. It was exhibited at the 1976 Commercial Motor Show in this blue and silver colour scheme, which, with the addition of advertising for 'fare cards', became the basis of the company's commemorative livery for the 1977 Silver Jubilee. Note on the right the former No. 2535 (370 MHU), an MW5G now numbered W21 in the 'works' fleet and equipped internally with a Gardner LX engine and generator. Precautions were being taken against power cuts at this time of 'industrial unrest'. The building in the background, Berkeley House, was now the company's head office. Inevitably, during these years, it became known to employees as 'Fawlty Towers'. The photograph was taken on Saturday 12 February 1977.

The last gasp of the KSWs. Muller Road's No. C8429 (YHT 925) is seen in Fishponds Road, operating (from Staple Hill depot) the 16.02 journey from New Cheltenham on the 55 service – historically the 4A – on Tuesday 28 October 1975. New in September 1957, the bus still carries Tilling livery, which has been adulterated by the addition of an NBC-style white band. It was withdrawn in March 1976. Bus shelters of that endearingly ugly concrete pattern have now vanished and the area behind the bus was demolished during the nineties for a Safeway supermarket.

Numerically the last of the Bristol 'city' services, the 99 was descended from a route started by Greyhound Motors, which was absorbed by Bristol Tramways in 1936. A list of services operating in 1949 gives it as Avonmouth–Prince Street, but by the time of the photograph, Monday 5 April 1976, the easterly terminus was at the Concorde public house in Stockwood. It ran only once every thirty minutes and was the only route that served two major thoroughfares in their entirety – Feeder Road and The Portway. The bus, FLF No. C7026 (821 MHW), seen here at Bath Bridge, had led an uneventful but blameless life since entering traffic in 1962, being always allocated to Winterstoke Road depot.

The MW had a gearbox incorporating rudimentary synchromesh. Probably because of the long linkages between the cab and the gearbox, which was under the floor amidships, the gearstick had a gluey, slow-motion feel often likened to stirring treacle. The vehicle was sufficiently unlike others for a special training bus to be set aside for 'familiarisation'. No. W157 (521 JHU) had entered service in November 1960 as bus No. 2999. It was withdrawn from the main fleet in October 1975 and is seen here, parked outside the paint shop at Lawrence Hill, on Thursday 26 January 1978. Oddly, its services were retained for some time after the last operational MWs had been withdrawn.

The early bus-bodied REs in the fleet had the shallower, 'frowning' windscreen that was designed to accommodate a 'T-box' destination display. This led to one of those unlooked-for consequences, in that the driver found himself on wet days trying to see through the unswept arc at the top edge of the windscreen. A makeshift solution has been attempted here by bending the wiper arm to bring the blade higher up. Later, the T-box was replaced by a side-by-side configuration, which made it possible to raise the top edge of the screen. Seen on Friday 3 February 1978, No. 1030 (MAE 33F) is posed on the switchback 358 service in Down Road, Portishead, on the 13.08 journey from Redcliffe Bay to Bristol.

A significant withdrawal on 31 July 1976 was that of No. C7000 (995 EHW), the prototype of the FLF Lodekka. It had been turned out by ECW in October 1959. After being demonstrated to a number of operators it was returned to ECW to have its sliding door replaced by the four-leaf folding door that became standard. Note the 'scroll' fleet name, in its NBC form, which disappeared after the dissolution of the Joint Services agreement with the city council in 1978. The bus was photographed at Lawrence Hill depot on Thursday 4 March 1976. A sympathetic passing inspector moved it forward so that I could get a better shot. The bus was eventually exported to the United States and is believed to survive in Hawaii.

Dual-door, forty-four-seat RELL No. G1152 (UHY 647H), of the Gloucester city fleet, was, to judge from its down-at-the-back look, being driven with some vigour when photographed on Saturday 8 January 1977. The shot was taken just around the corner from Gloucester's bus station and the building jutting out from the left-hand edge was the staff canteen. The meandering service linking Bristol to Gloucester, via Wootton-under-Edge and Dursley, was a particular favourite of mine and I've downed a few cups of its vending machine coffee in my time.

Looking very spruce for a bus new in 1961 and four days short of its withdrawal, No. 6024 (726 JHY) is seen at Lawrence Hill depot on Friday 27 August 1976. Service 'revisions' – which, being interpreted, meant reductions – at the end of June had led to a bumper crop of withdrawals, including the first of the forward-entrance vehicles. By the following week there were only two FSFs left on the road in Bristol; however, a handful survived in Bath into 1977.

There was a time when superannuated buses were often to be found among the tractor units, generating sets and caravans that huddled around fairgrounds and travelling circuses. A noteworthy example was BHW 432, which had started life in 1935 as No. JNW70, a Bristol J-type with four-cylinder 'NW' petrol engine. During the war it had been fitted with perimeter seating to increase standing room. In 1946 it received a five-cylinder Gardner LW engine, becoming a JO5G, and three years later it was rebodied by ECW and fitted with the PV2 radiator we see here. It was withdrawn from service in 1959. It is seen on Sunday 2 April 1978 on Rodway Hill, Mangotsfield.

An isolated RELL, No. 1049, was delivered with a new moquette seating fabric and brighter internal colour-scheme, visible from outside in the grey instrument binnacle; from No. 1061 onwards this became the standard interior décor. For a while the T-box destination screen and shallow windscreen were retained, as demonstrated by No. 1088 (OHY 518F). Delivered in 1968 as a single-door fifty-three-seater, it was returned within a year to ECW for conversion to a dual-door forty-four-seater. Dual-door single-deckers rapidly fell out of favour at the end of the 1970s, when a policy of service cuts and fleet reductions entailed packing more passengers into fewer vehicles.

In 1964 British Leyland acquired a shareholding in Bristol Commercial Vehicles. The marriage was consummated, so to speak, by the availability to Bristol vehicles of a Leyland engine option. Bristol's No. 7129 (822 SHW) was the first FLF Lodekka constructed for any operator with Leyland's 0.600 engine; the two that followed went to the 'city' fleet, but No. 7129 was always allocated to Bath. It was rarely seen in Bristol, but on Tuesday 19 September 1976 was photographed in Keynsham on the main 339 service between the two cities.

The KS was a lengthened version of the K-type, which had been in production since 1936. In 1951 it was decided to take advantage of recent changes to the Construction and Use Regulations by fitting 8-foot-wide bodies to 7-foot 6-inch chassis then on the production line. The resultant hybrids are sometimes given as KS(W). With the chassis also constructed to 8 feet, the model became the KSW. No. 8022 (NAE 54) had been new in 1951 and was withdrawn in May 1968. It became a mobile stores and workshop, and then, in October 1970, an engineering training bus, numbered W136. It is recorded as finally being withdrawn in May 1975, but was still to be found in the yard of Lawrence Hill depot on Monday 10 October 1977.

Beyond the wooden Wayfarers pub was the lonely terminus of Bristol's 'killer road' the 88 – historically the 8 and probably the busiest of the 'city' services. Under the long grass on either side of the road were the footings of old cottages, for this had been the village of Charlton, which was evacuated in the 1950s when the Bristol Aeroplane Co. wanted to extend the Filton runway for its Brabazon aeroplane – a kind of Jumbo before its time. In the seventies, the turning place at the end of the road made an excellent vantage point, from which bus crews could observe the taxi-trials of the production Concordes as they were turned out from the neighbouring hangars. Bristol-engined FLF No. C7096 (541 OHU) awaits departure on Friday 10 September 1976.

The company acquired three Land Rovers in February 1973, which were numbered W10–12 in the 'works' fleet. Two at least were ex-military. The canvas top of this vehicle has a military look, but since I stupidly threw away the original print of the photograph, on the reverse of which I would have recorded details, I am not able to give a definite identification. On Monday 19 June 1978 it was parked at Lawrence Hill 'awaiting spares', according to a sticker in the windscreen. To judge from the towbar and buffer plate, it had been adapted as a tug, and was probably used for shunting stricken buses around the yard.

All deliveries of REs until October 1970 had been powered by Leyland 0.680 engines. In that month, No. C1180 (YAE 443J) was exhibited at the Commercial Motor Show but didn't enter service until the following June, by which time it had acquired a Leyland 0.500 engine. Five more REs fitted with Leyland's 'fixed-head wonder' went into traffic at the same time and were allocated to Winterstoke Road depot. I would conjecture that this was linked to development of the Leyland National, which eventually went into production with a turbocharged version of the same engine. The bus is seen in Stapleton Road on Sunday 10 July 1977. Note the small '0.500' badge in the corner of the radiator grille.

The Bristol SU was a shameless counterfeit of the Albion Nimbus which, for political reasons, was not available to Tilling fleets. Only 181 were built and, of those, 133 were taken by a single company, Western National. Twenty-five of the total were of the short (SUS) variant, of which Bristol had nine. All but two had been disposed of by 1971; these were put to work on local services at Nailsworth. No. 303 (843 THY) waits on Friday 16 December 1977 for its 14.33 departure from Tiltup's End, where the turning place was the forecourt of a garage.

The Bristol 'city' services reached suburbs, such as Patchway, Downend and Kingswood, which were beyond the city's boundary in Gloucestershire. Mileage operated beyond the boundary by 'city' fleet buses had to be balanced for accounting purposes. Accordingly, there was always a minority of 'country' fleet buses on 'city' routes. For some reason probably connected with the Hanham Local Services inherited from W. Bence in 1936, the outer suburbs of Oldland and Cadbury Heath retained a 'country' service of their own. On Thursday 9 December 1976 an FLF6B on the 388 service is seen in Clarence Road, Easton. To further confuse matters the bus, No. C7139 (832 SHW), belongs to the 'city' fleet.

The tobacco factories of Messrs W. D. & H. O. Wills, spread over several sites in Bedminster, Southville and Ashton, generated their own rush hours: there was even a mini-rush hour at lunchtime, for which special buses were laid on. At noon on Tuesday 15 January 1980, RELL No. 1239 (AHU 731J) is seen loading up in Raleigh Road, Southville. Before entering service in 1971 this bus was inspected by Colchester Corporation. Evidently they were impressed, placing substantial orders over the next few years for Bristol-style RELLs with Leyland 0.680 engines.

The earliest forward-entrance Lodekkas had continued the numbers of the rear-entrance LD and FS types, and this Bristol-engined FSF had entered service in 1960 as No. LC8568. The L stood for 'lowbridge' and was dropped once 'highbridge' types had been eliminated; the 8XXX numbers originally signified '8 feet wide'. With the introduction of the forward-entrance types it became difficult for allocators to know the seating capacities of the buses they were allocating and it was decided to introduce 60XX numbers for the sixty-seat FSF and the 70XX series for the FLF. Following its withdrawal in June 1976, No. C6010 (709 JHY) was acquired by Odstock Hospital, Salisbury, as a staff bus. Still carrying its 'city' fleet number, it is seen on Monday 22 May 1978 outside Salisbury General Hospital. Note the inevitable 999 route number.

The company thought it prudent, in view of contemporary industrial problems and anxieties concerning the supply of oil, to purchase a couple of second-hand bowsers with which it could move supplies of fuel between depots. Taken into the works fleet as No. W176, VMB 513J was an E. R. F. 64GX tractor unit that had been new in 1972. It was acquired with a flatbed trailer, but by the time of the photograph, taken at the Central Repair Works, Lawrence Hill, on Thursday 7 June 1979, it had been united with a tanker.

Into service on 1 November 1965, and withdrawn on 31 July 1980, Gardner-engined FLF No. 7224 (EHT 113C) is seen in London Road, Gloucester, on Tuesday 6 January 1976, a couple of minutes into its journey on the fifteen-minute headway service to Cheltenham. In September 1974 it was provided with extra luggage space, at the expense of two seats in the lower saloon. An interesting selection of contemporary motors in the street and in the yard of the second-hand car dealer.

The poetry of English place-names. Famous for its fare stage, Belmont Crossroads was between Cambridge Batch and Wraxall (Battle Axes Hotel). During the week, the 07.15 journey on the 364 service from Nailsea would have had a respectable load, but on Saturdays there were usually only one or two early shop workers; on Saturday 15 July 1978, RELL No. 1051 (MHW 855F) was completely empty. I used to wonder how much it had cost we ratepayers to have a man sent out with a van to paint out the initials of Somerset County Council from the little pyramidal finials on every signpost in the southerly part of the new 'county' of Avon.

The first of the refurbished LSs (see the earlier picture of No. 3000) was not externally modified, but the remainder were subjected to the frontal disfigurement we see here. This was unfortunate, since the LS had been a notably handsome vehicle. New in 1957, No. 3006 (YHY 74) was rebuilt in 1971 and is seen on Friday 18 November 1977 in Rodford Way, operating one of the Yate town services. Many drivers refused point-blank to operate one of the routes because of problems with parked cars in residential roads, and reports concerning 'Yate's phantom bus service' began to appear in the local newspapers. Like every driver I grumbled about the 'Yate locals', but secretly I quite liked them.

As recorded in the Introduction, I did not get off to a good start with 'the Radstocks'. In spite of this inauspicious beginning, I grew to like them. There were basically three services from Bristol, with one continuing to Frome, with peak-hour, school and weekend variants. One took a certain satisfaction in one's knowledge of the permutations. Usually a bus worked out as one service and returned as another. On Monday 5 April 1976, MW5G No. 2616 (CHY 409C) makes its way in along Bath Road on the 365 from Radstock, via Midsomer Norton, High Littleton, Farmborough and Keynsham.

Every route needed a lurking place and I cannily identified this small lay-by between Cold Ashton and Marshfield on this, my very first journey as a one-man driver. It was the 06.57 departure from Bristol on the 335 service to Marshfield on Monday 23 May 1977. By waiting here, rather than going around to the terminus, you avoided sitting for ten minutes with two or three old dears staring at the back of your head, making little 'tut' sounds as they consulted their wristwatches. The bus, No. 2408 (BHW 96C), was an MW5G ordered by Eastern National and delivered to Bristol in Eastern National livery, registered JHK 462C.

Bristol's first REs were RELH coaches, which entered service in the Bristol Greyhound coach fleet in 1963–4. This had been No. 2133 (979 WAE). Still a schoolboy, I remember how modern, almost futuristic, they seemed. A write-up appeared in the *Bristol Evening Post*. During a demonstration run on the M50 near Ross-on-Wye (which, at the time, must have been the nearest available motorway) a brimming cup of tea was placed on the floor of the speeding coach. Not a drop spilled, wrote the *Post*'s man. Well... perhaps. The coaches had manual gearboxes. The whole batch passed to Western National in 1974. When photographed at Canon's Marsh, Bristol, on Saturday 12 August 1978, the coach belonged to Morris Brothers of Swansea.

The hamlet of Sheperdine, on the English bank of the Severn, used to benefit from a bus service consisting of two return journeys on Wednesday mornings. Loadings were erratic, but were occasionally 'standing room only'. The busy journeys were those that brought the villagers in to Thornbury to do their shopping and took them home afterwards; these, of course, were balanced by two 'dead' journeys. RESL No. 509 (THU 355G) is seen on Wednesday 12 July 1978 beneath the church of St Arild's, which overlooks the estuary from a monticle above the village of Oldbury-on-Severn.

A pair of Bristol-engined FLF Lodekkas at Lawrence Hill depot on Saturday 2 July 1977. The closest is immediately recognisable, by its non-contemporary radiator grille, as No. 7114 (807 SHW); the other is No. 7194 (CHT 537C). Both buses display the 339 service number and belonged to Marlborough Street depot. Coach movements caused serious congestion in the bus station on summer weekends, but with fewer buses required than on weekdays it was possible to park surplus vehicles at Lawrence Hill. Buses were parked here front-outwards to save the residents of Tyndall Road from the noise of early morning starts.

Two chassis parked at the Central Repair Works on Friday 23 March 1979. That on the left was No. RELL3/167, from bus No. 1022 (MAE 25F), whose body had been scrapped after an accident. Chassis parts were donated to another casualty, No. C1134 (UHY 629H). On the right is an LH chassis, No. LH326, from Hants & Dorset's No. 1526 (RLJ 790H). An interesting assortment of 1970s cars in the background belonging to CRW staff. Every day, every driver heard the old chestnut, 'If the fares were lower more people would travel and your company would make more money.' I sometimes used to drawl that if you took this argument to its logical conclusion the company would make the most money by charging nothing. My sledgehammer argument, though, was to indicate the staff car park at the entrance to the bus station and point out that all the cars belonged to company staff, who could travel free on buses.

Another K-type from the staff bus fleet of Brains Foods. This had been a Bristol-engined example, new in 1948 as Bristol Tramways No. C3435 (LHU 982). It was withdrawn in 1965 and acquired by Brains in the November of that year. It is thought to have been used until November 1969. Evidently it was retained as a source of spares and on Sunday 28 August 1977 was to be found abandoned on this patch of waste ground on the Brains site, up to its axles in summer grass, stripped even of its body panels.

Not many are about, understandably, on Friday 16 February 1979, during what was a notably snowy winter. Five years before Wells Road had been lined with shops serving an area of closely packed Victorian streets. The city council had cleared the houses for a road interchange whose construction is awaited to the present day. The 30-group services fanned out from Wells Road to reach south Bristol's post-war housing estates and were a monopoly of the dual-door RELLs. No. 1178 (YAE 441J) climbs out of the city towards Bridge Farm Estate.

Gardner-engined LD No. L8394 (WHY 947) had been new in 1956 and was withdrawn on the last day of 1972. It was taken inside for rebuilding as an open-topper and received this impressive paint scheme. They were planning ahead, for 1973 would be the 600th anniversary of the charter that granted Bristol its county status. Renumbered as L8582, the bus re-entered service on a commemorative sightseeing route, numbered (of course) 600. It was continued the following year and, by the date of the photograph, Friday 27 August 1976, had become the 'Open-Top Circular'.

When Bristol absorbed the local services in Gloucester in 1934, it was agreed that the city's buses should remain a separate entity within the fleet and continue to carry the Gloucester name and coat of arms. Distinctions of this kind, and deference to local allegiances, were to become a thing of the past. Seen in Southgate Street on Wednesday 24 May 1978, VRT No. G5089 (NHU 672R) was a little over a year old. The Bristol company was unusual in owning large numbers of dual-door VRTs, whose stairs and lower deck seating layout were most unsatisfactory.

Bus termini, of their nature, tend to be at the extremity of things. Lonely roads on council estates, windy lay-bys and concrete bus shelters adjoining ranks of suburban shops fallen on decline. Few were more dismal than the Southmead terminus of the 88. On Sunday 19 September 1976 the turning space looked relatively tidy, but fly tipping was a constant problem and reversals were often obstructed by Draylon sofas or lengths of shag-pile carpet. Because of outbreaks of 'trouble' in Southmead, the 88 was now worked on evenings and Sundays by radio-equipped, crewed REs. This nearside view of Gardner-engined No. C1281 (EAE 684K) shows the barcode scanner window and transmitter 'fin' associated with the Marconi 'B-Line' bus location system.

AEC Matador ex-military gun tractors were a popular choice among bus operators for conversion to towing wagons. Bristol owned several, including three with this rather bulbous company-made bodywork. The windscreen has a distinct contemporary PSV look and the radiator grille mimics that of a Lodekka. In company parlance they were always known as 'Jumbos' and spent most of their time towing stricken buses back to their home depots on rigid tow, although a Harvey-Frost 5-ton crane was provided for occasions when suspended tow was necessary. No. W109, carrying trade plate 525 HT, was photographed at Lawrence Hill on Monday 8 October 1979.

A survivor from the company's first batch of MWs, the former No. 2938 (928 AHY) had entered service in 1958. This earlier style of bodywork for the MW was not well received. There was no provision for a cream band under the windows, meaning that the relief colour had to be applied to the window surrounds. Subsequent re-styling rectified the matter and also corrected the rather unsightly back end. The bus was photographed at Pembroke Dock on Saturday 13 August 1977, by which time it belonged to the renowned local independent, Silcox – a large user of second-hand Bristols, many from the Bristol fleet. An ex-Hants & Dorset MW brings up the rear.

Even before the great minibus brainstorm of the eighties and early nineties, the company had operated a small number of such vehicles for certain specialised services. No. 300 (XAE 965H) was a petrol-engined Ford Transit with bodywork by H. G. Strachan, used on a service catering to the tourist trade in Bath. It had replaced a fondly remembered Trojan, which had come from Silver Star Motor Services of Porton Down. Behind is No. 301 (PHU 647M), a Leyland Redline 440EA, introduced at Gloucester in 1973, but used in various roles during its later years. The pair is seen on Saturday 8 December 1979, laid up for the winter in the shed at Lawrence Hill.

Not a few 'time expired' buses went on to find further use during the 'Playbus' fad of the 1970s. The former No. 7159 (AAE 264B), a Gardner-engined FLF Lodekka, had spent most of its life working from Stroud. When seen in Canon's Road, Bristol, on Saturday 19 May 1979, it seemed to be suffering from dermatitis, but was later to acquire a Fisher-Price colour scheme of strident primary hues. The mighty tobacco bonds were to be felled in 1988 as the area was made ready for redevelopment.

The 07.44 departure from Bristol on the 311 service was mainly provided for schools. It continued beyond the usual terminus to Castle School, Thornbury, and turned off en route to serve Marlwood School, Alveston. LH No. 375 (KHU 325P) is seen, on Friday 17 February 1978, in Quarry Road, Alveston, shortly after calling at Marlwood. The bus went on to spend the rest of the morning on a charming group of services known as the 'Thornbury Locals', which linked that small town, 12 miles north of Bristol, to villages in the Vale of Berkeley. None of this survived the carnage of rural services that followed the MAP project.

Another doomed service was the 315, which connected Fishponds with Yate via Downend, Kendleshire and Winterbourne Down. RELL No. 1107 (SHW 129G) was one of the first batch with side-by-side destination display and deeper windscreen. From a visibility point of view, this was an improvement, but it somewhat spoiled the vehicle's looks. They still hadn't got it quite right. The route number was on the nearside and its winding mechanism almost out of reach; all subsequent deliveries had the numbers on the offside, making the five members of the 'SHW' batch always identifiable from a distance. The location, seen on Saturday 29 July 1978, was between Downend and Kendleshire, with the M4 motorway bridged just behind the bus.

The third of Bristol's trio of Leyland-engined FLFs, No. 7131 (824 SHW), is seen approaching the city centre from Rupert Street on Saturday 27 May 1978. Note that the bus is in 'withdrawn' condition, without advertising, fleet name or fleet number plate: it had been reinstated to cover a shortage of vehicles. This may have been connected with a dispute, mainly affecting Muller Road depot, involving the lack of power-assisted steering in early VRTs. Amid reports of muscle strains and slipped discs, they were taken out of service for modification. No. 7131 went on to serve until May 1979.

This engaging little vehicle, not much bigger than a fairground dodgem car, was a Clark 'Clarktor 6' tractor. They were made, 1940–49, by the Clark Equipment Co. of Chicago and were mainly used as aircraft tugs. The USAF owned large numbers. The Bristol company acquired this example in 1948 and it was numbered W41 in the 'works' fleet. It must have spent most of its time indoors as a bus shunter at the Central Repair Works. This occasion, Thursday 25 October 1979, was the only time I saw it in the open air.

Five-cylinder Gardner-powered MW No. 2595 (988 UHW) is posed on the 07.16 departure from Bristol on the 333 service to Doynton on Saturday 2 July 1977. Doynton is a village nestled under the Cotswold escarpment close to the foot of Tog Hill. The photograph was taken in the little lane that connects it to the main A420 Bristol–Chippenham road. The bus had entered service in March 1964 and spent its days between Marlborough Street, Weston-super-Mare, Wells and Lawrence Hill depots. It was withdrawn on the last day of September 1978 and was scrapped in March 1979 by a breaker at Carlton, near Barnsley.

Falling snow seldom photographs well. The evenly descending, half crown-sized flakes you remember become scruffy-looking wind-blown specks and the photograph looks as though it came from a dusty negative. When I took this shot, outside Hanham depot on Thursday 15 February 1979, Bristol City Council had recently relinquished its half ownership of the Bristol Joint Services; this implied the assimilation of the Hanham local services and the closure of their depot. Dual-door RELL No. 1194 (THU 514J) awaits a fresh driver on Hanham's trunk service, the 380 to Downend. The depot closed on 3 October 1981, with staff and services transferring to Marlborough Street.

Having gone to the trouble of fitting FLF No. C7255 (FHW 160D) with a Gardner LW engine in place of its original Bristol BVW, the company was prevailed upon, in March 1978, to pass the bus to the Avon & Somerset Constabulary for use as a mobile crime prevention exhibition. It didn't pass through a dealer and was prepared and repainted by the company. Judging by the speed at which it once passed me on the Keynsham bypass (the uniformed police driver fraternally waving), I think a five-speed gearbox must have been fitted and the engine 'opened up' a little. The bus proceeds along Temple Way in a southerly direction on Thursday 22 June 1978.

One of the company's five-strong batch of 'flat windscreen' dual-purpose RELHs, No. 2057 (TAE 418G) approaches Swindon bus station on Thursday 1 November 1979. It appears that the bus will next be working a journey to Malmesbury. The 419 service had once continued through to Bristol, but had been severed at Malmesbury two years before. It is believed that county council subsidy was unforthcoming for the through service.

Not universally well received by the operating side of the industry, the Leyland National underwent a number of modifications in its early years. Its tendency to 'roll' was remedied and the batteries were re-positioned over the front axle to correct a propensity of the front wheels to skid when cornering on wet roads. The 'B-Series' offered a lower-spec. version with conventional heating (eliminating the characteristic roof 'pod'), simplified interior lighting and a de-rated engine. There was no left-hand drive version and the vehicle was available only in 10.3-metre form. No. 712 (XEU 860T) is seen at Lawrence Hill depot on Saturday 28 July 1979, when newly delivered.

Another of the company's imposing ex-military AEC Matador towing wagons, still carrying its admirably spartan Ministry of Supply bodywork. Carrying Wiltshire-issued trade plate 109 MR, No. W141 was pictured at Lawrence Hill depot, presumably on some errand from its Swindon base, on Friday 3 December 1976.

The 'Thornbury Locals': more like a week's touring holiday than work. Tuesdays and Thursdays were the same, but the other days of the week brought variety. 10.3-metre Leyland National No. 554 (GEU 366N) is posed at Grovesend, near Tytherington, on Friday 14 July 1978. The housing estates of Thornbury slumber in the distance and the A38 road crosses left–right behind the bus. It was a ten-minute trip, but the next journey went through to Yate, via Itchington, Latteridge and Iron Acton.

Perhaps no driver had obligingly driven a bus under the railway bridge in Gipsy Patch Lane lately. When the time came to replace the ageing fleet of FS open-toppers at Weston-super-Mare, the company acquired a number of second-hand vehicles and modified them intentionally. The future No. 8603 (HOR 589E) had come from the Hants & Dorset fleet, but had been new in 1967 to a well-known independent, R. Chisnell (King Alfred) of Winchester. It was a Roe-bodied Leyland Atlantean PDR1/2 and is seen here being made ready at the Central Repair Works on Thursday 7 June 1979.

On the city services in Bristol, the men's union insisted upon dual-door vehicles for use on one-man routes. Elsewhere this was not thought necessary, and the company ordered the conventional single-door versions of the Bristol VRT found almost everywhere else. Seen in Fleming Way, Swindon, on Saturday 14 January 1978, No. 5515 (LHT 725P) was one of a minority of VRTs in the fleet powered by the Leyland 0.501 engine. Converted to an open-topper, the bus is believed to survive on sightseeing work in Canada.

RELL No. 1166 (XAE 486H) was the first supplied to the company with the curved 'BET' windscreen imposed by the National Bus Company. The curve added 5 inches to the vehicle's overall length and, in my view, spoiled its appearance. The 50-group services that converged upon Fishponds Road from various termini in the north-east suburbs were worked by Staple Hill depot with the exception of the 51, which was provided from Lawrence Hill. The photograph was taken at the Queensholm Drive, Bromley Heath, terminus on Saturday 22 March 1980.

The eight Bristol-engined FLFs that were transferred to the Bristol fleet when Western National's Trowbridge enclave was handed over were given fleet numbers following those of Bristol's own. Thus, No. 7321 (EDV 511D) became, numerically, the last FLF in the fleet – though far from the newest. The rest of the batch eventually gravitated to Bath, but 7321 remained a Trowbridge bus until it was withdrawn in April 1978. The side-by-side destination screens and outside winding handles were unique to this batch. The bus is seen operating one of the Chippenham 'town' services on Wednesday 18 May 1977.

LH No. 375 (KHU 325P) is seen on Thursday 21 June 1979 at Newport, on the A38 between Bristol and Gloucester. A driver I knew was sitting in his bus at Bristol bus station one day, waiting to leave for Gloucester. A passenger approached: 'D'you go to Newport', he asked. Yes he did, said the driver. The man paid his fare and sat down. When he got there the driver, remembering that someone had asked for Newport, pulled in at the kerb. He turned and caught the passenger's eye: 'Here you are,' he said. The man stared around at the pub, the few houses and the hedges and pastures that stretched in all directions beyond. Somewhere nearby a cow lowed. Of course, he'd wanted Newport, Gwent. All the driver could suggest was that he continue to Gloucester and ride back to Bristol to connect with the last bus to Cardiff. As he arrived back in Bristol, deliberately early, the Cardiff bus was loading up. By this time the passenger needed to use the toilet and disappeared into the facility on the bus station's platform. While he was inside, the Cardiff bus departed. The driver, who had now finished work, paid in his takings and left by a little-used side entrance.

RELL No. 1139 (UHY 634H) entered service on 1 December 1969 and spent its first years allocated to Brislington depot. It had been at Winterstoke Road depot since October 1971. The 59 service was the descendent of the 9, which, in 1970, had been one of the earliest conversions to one-man operation of a bread-and-butter cross-city route. The bus was pictured on Friday 2 May 1980 in the busy and congested Church Road, Redfield.

An elegant PSV-to-towing wagon conversion was performed in 1973 on MW6G No. 2113 (406 LHT), a former coach that was new in 1961 to the company's Bristol Greyhound fleet. The Greyhound name perpetuated that of a rival operator bought out by Bristol Tramways in 1936. The vehicle is seen standing by for a call upon its services at Lawrence Hill on Monday 8 October 1979.

Withdrawn and out of use awaiting disposal at Lawrence Hill on Saturday 15 July 1978 were these near twins, formerly of the Bristol Greyhound coach fleet. Both were MW6Gs new in April 1965. They were downgraded to bus status when their recertification overhauls became due at seven years. No. 2427 (BHU 93C), the bus furthest from the camera, had been fitted with a new engine only weeks before being withdrawn, and someone has clearly appropriated the winged Bristol-ECW badge from the front of No. 2429 (BHU 93C). The company had not replaced the coach seats and red interior trim at the time of downgrading and must have kept a set of unique one-line destination blinds for this small batch of vehicles.

The REs of the Bristol fleet, in their various forms, were mainly powered by Leyland 0.680 engines. The most numerous exceptions to this rule were fourteen RELLs diverted from Western National, which had ordered Gardner HLX engines. I was always rather glad that there were no more. Although the Gardner was a superbly engineered engine and had an excellent reputation, the Leyland was much the nicer 'drive'. One of the diverted Western National vehicles, No. 1283 (EAE 686K), is seen on Tuesday 15 January 1980, in Ilminster Avenue, Knowle West, operating the circuitous 36 service.

It was coming down in stair rods on the afternoon of Wednesday 22 March 1978 as MW5G No. 2405 (BHW 93C) waited outside the Railway Hotel in Station Road, Yate. The road rises in the distance to cross the old Midland main line from Bristol to Gloucester. The bus was probably waiting to operate a journey provided for Parnall's factory, then manufacturing Creda 'white goods'. It was one of those ordered by Eastern National but diverted to Bristol. It was withdrawn nine days after the photograph was taken, but went on to serve as a staff bus for Lockwood's Foods of Long Sutton, Lincolnshire.

VRT No. 5084 (NFB 120R), photographed under cover in the shed at Lawrence Hill on Monday 8 October 1979. The account I heard was that in leaving Avonmouth depot early one morning, the driver (who did not for long afterwards remain employed by the company) absent-mindedly turned left instead of right. He attempted to rectify his error by turning in the forecourt of a garage, but in his haste failed to notice, or omitted from his calculations, the canopy over the petrol pumps, with the lamentable result we see here. The bus went on to be fully repaired: at only two and a half years old, it was too new to be 'pensioned off' as an open-topper at Weston.

According to the *Evening Post*'s usually reliable clock, it was 13.19 and 16°C. With most of the bus's sliding vents open, there must have been a touch of spring in the air on Friday 6 April 1979. Winterstoke Road depot's Bristol-engined FLF No. 7187 (BHU 980C) noses out onto the Old Market roundabout, Henbury-bound on the 77 service. The driver of the Dodge flatbed lorry is to be commended on the excellence of his roping and sheeting – a skill now lost to the road haulage industry. All that part of the *Post* building behind the bus has since been demolished.

It was Thursday 24 May 1979. Long hair on young men and 'flared' trousers – both fashions dating from the sixties – had had a good run. On the opposite side of Rupert Street, 'four star' was 89p per gallon. Closely followed by one of Staple Hill's Leyland Nationals on the Fishponds Road 'corridor', VRT No. 5006 (EHU 365K) heads for Knowle West on the 71, descended from a route established by Greyhound Motors. Note the advertisements for the Carrefour 'hypermarket' at Cribbs Causeway – a great local sensation when it opened, but nowadays, as the Asda Wal-Mart Supercentre, it is of unexceptional size.

Hinton and Dyrham, just beyond Bristol's easterly suburbs, received a bus once a week on Thursdays. Reversals were necessary at both villages and the authorised place at Hinton was the car park of the Bull Inn. Deluxe accommodation was provided on the morning of Thursday 3 April 1980: RELH No. 2084 (NHW 313F) had entered service as a Greyhound coach and, albeit that it had been downgraded to dual-purpose status, retained its coach seating and agreeable red upholstery. The date was a locally significant one, for it was the morning after the St Pauls riots and the bus would be making its way back to Bristol through the blackened and brick-strewn wreckage of Sussex Place. Copycat disturbances followed in other cities, notably at Toxteth, Liverpool.

Sheperdine receives its weekly bus, provided, on Wednesday 24 January 1979, by 10.3-metre Leyland National No. 555 (GEU 367N). The bus runs out of road as it encounters the River Severn and turns in the car park of a public house. Most of the passengers boarded at Oldbury-on-Severn, but along the route farmer's wives waited at the ends of their lanes, or elderly maiden sisters, shopping bags at the ready, stood at the gates of crumbling seventeenth-century cottages. The snow had fallen at the weekend, partially melting in the sun during the ensuing days. The short-wheelbase National was not, perhaps, the bus you'd have chosen in which to drive on knobbly, thrice re-frozen slush.

Battling through the snow on Thursday 15 February 1979, FLF6G No. 7170 approaches Park Crescent, Cadbury Heath, known locally, for reasons lost in the mists of antiquity, as 'Banjo Island'. The bus had spent most of its life as a 'G-prefix' Gloucester city vehicle, but was now serving out its last days at Hanham and Lawrence Hill, probably in connection with mileage-balancing. With the ending of the Bristol Joint Services agreement the 388 service was to disappear in the following October, grafted onto extended 'city' routes.

An interior view of an RELL, taken from my favourite rear offside corner seat. The bus was operating Hanham's 380 service. We are in Downend Road, Kingswood; up ahead are the traffic lights where Soundwell Road begins. Unfortunately the number of the bus went unrecorded. There are no very helpful clues: this was an off-the-peg, dual-door, forty-four-seater with BET curved screen and four-leaf folding doors. I never liked this lighter interior décor: I preferred the gloomy dark green rexine of the early REs. The date was Saturday 13 September 1980.

The company acquired this Leyland Retriever 22LRT/3AR in 1972 as a six-wheel tipper chassis registered LEH 247E. Converted to a recovery vehicle, it was numbered W142 and carried trade plate 176 HT. When the photograph was taken on Wednesday 16 January 1980, it had just left Muller Road depot with an FLF Lodekka in tow, probably being taken to Lawrence Hill for a repair.

Another of the former Bristol Greyhound six-cylinder MW coaches which were downgraded to bus (not even dual-purpose) status but retained a full complement of red coach seats. They were always identifiable by their 'letterbox' destination screens and the absence of a separate route number. No. 2432 (BHU 96C) had been new in April 1965 and was withdrawn 31 January 1979, but was loaned throughout the January and February of that year to South Wales Transport, which explains the Swansea destination. These matters moved slowly and on Thursday 7 June 1979 the bus was still awaiting disposal at Lawrence Hill.

No. G7269 (HAE 278D) was so rudely snatched from its accustomed haunts on the Gloucester city services that it was pressed into traffic in Bristol before there'd been a chance of removing its GLOUCESTER fleet name and G-prefix number. It ran in this condition for several months. The photo was taken in Colston Avenue on the morning of Friday 27 June 1980, the day after its transfer. The waiting passenger looks like an employee of BAC or Rolls-Royce, on his way to one of the aero factories in Filton or Patchway. These passengers were not always popular with bus crews. They were, perhaps, a little too aware of their status as the aristocracy of the skilled working class. They were great moaners and tireless writers of complaining letters.

Seen against a vanished background, RESL No. 511 (THU 357G) loads up in Railway Street, Bath, on Saturday 28 April 1979. The 1950s bus station across the street and Owen Luder's Southgate Shopping Centre, in the background, have both disappeared in recent years. The bus, too, was living on borrowed time. It was withdrawn at the end of September at only ten years old, but went on to see further service with South Wales Transport.

The LHW and MHW L-registered VRTs were always identifiable from a distance by their grey window-sealing rubber – used for a while by ECW but, fortunately, soon discontinued. Most of the early VRTs came to be fitted with the vile CAV488 automatic transmission. This was often referred to as an 'automatic gearbox': in fact the gearbox was a standard unit; the CAV system sensed the rotation speed of the propeller shaft and initiated gearchanges automatically at the appropriate speed. In the trade press automatic transmission was referred to as though the answer to every driver's prayers. I never encountered a driver with a good word to say for it. No. 5019 (MHW 286L) awaits attention at CRW on Thursday 7 June 1979.

There was always a minority of withdrawn buses that went on to enjoy a second career, usually of short duration, in some ancillary employment. MW5G No. 2418 (HAE 262D) had been new in June 1966 with dual-purpose seating, removed in 1973. Following its withdrawal at the end of April 1979 it was modified as a mobile office. Its future works number, W28, is marked on the windscreen in CRW yellow chalk, with what looks like a job number. It was snapped behind Berkeley House on Monday 8 October 1979. Note the mast and coil of cable behind the entrance door, for the provision of electrical supply.

All these things are matter of taste, but I always thought this the most elegant coach body of its time. Even so, RELH No. 2083 (NHW 312F) was, by Saturday 26 August 1978, getting on a bit for front line express coach duties. It had been downgraded and repainted into dual-purpose livery three years before, but a vehicle shortage forced its return to express duties. National Express management discouraged the use of 'buses' on coach duties and the vehicle was painted back into National white. It subsequently returned to dual-purpose condition. The vehicle is seen at Gordano Services, on the M5 motorway at the south end of the Avonmouth bridge.

An early RELL, No. 1005 (LAE 340E), stands with a brand new LH and several freshly delivered VRTs at the Central Repair Works on Tuesday 2 March 1976. The new buses were being made ready for service: the only identifiable VRT, No. 5505 (KOU 791P) entered traffic at Bath on 1 May. On the right a party of senior engineering types discuss high policy.

In 1980 the company began to receive the Leyland National 2. This particular example, No. 3525 (BHY 999V), was the test bed for a new transmission made by ZF (Zahradfabrik Friedrichshaven), which became a standard fitting in British buses and coaches. It would happily cruise along at 65 mph, which made it ideal for the semi-coach role; it was later fitted with dual-purpose seating. The next bus of this batch, No. 3526, received the registration BOU 1V – the first time the changeover between two marques had occurred within a single batch, and the company's first 'one' registration since NAE 1 (an L-type coach) in 1950. The bus is seen newly delivered on Saturday 6 September 1980.

Flat front, side-by-side destination screen, two-panel exit door, single headlights: the ECW bodywork of REs underwent considerable variation and all these features changed. No. 1128 (UHY 623H) lacks a two-letter depot code before its fleet number, probably because it belonged to the 'Traffic Pool', an unallocated reserve of vehicles that led a nomadic existence between depots to cover for shortages. The 10 service was operated from Winterstoke Road depot but the driver was a Lawrence Hill man – probably a 'grabber' (one voluntarily working overtime) or a spare man at the Centre. The photo was taken at Inns Court Green on Tuesday 15 January 1980.

A line-up of old and new in the rank at the back of Manvers Street bus station, Bath, on Thursday 24 March 1977. Closest to the camera was VRT No. 5509 (KOU 795P), which had entered service less than a year before. Behind that were three MW5Gs, Nos 2554, 2565 and 2629. Bringing up the rear were two FLF Lodekkas, Bristol-engined No. 7142 and Gardner-engined No. 7242. The bus station was opened in 1958, but the building was replaced in 2009.

After fourteen years in the Cheltenham District Traction fleet, FLF No. 7276 (HHW 459D) found itself suddenly transplanted to the city services in Bristol. These 'mileage balancing' reallocations late in a vehicle's life usually signified an early appointment with the oxy-acetylene torch, but this bus lasted a further three years and is thought to survive in France. The photograph shows it in Cock Road, Kingswood, late in the afternoon on Friday 9 May 1980, still with its CHELTENHAM fleet name. Rather unprofessionally the driver opens the doors while the bus is still moving and the passenger, who must have just knocked off and been looking forward to his weekend, gets ready to hit the ground running.

The car park at Canon's Marsh, a stone's throw from Bristol's city centre, was used to hold buses 'off the road' if drivers were not available. I would guess that a driver had just been found to work this bus forward as overtime. An inspector is in attendance, giving instructions on where to resume service. The bus, No. 1400 (JHU 841L), seen on Saturday 14 October 1978, was the company's first Leyland National. It had been licensed in January 1973 for driver training and was one of ten that entered service on 25 February. It was fitted from new with ZF fully automatic transmission. The interesting early ferro-concrete structure in the background had been a goods shed serving the city docks.

KSWs continued to serve as training buses for some years after the type had disappeared from the revenue-earning fleet. The former No. C8407 (YHT 903), a Bristol AVW-engined example, had been withdrawn in October 1973 and was re-licensed for training, numbered W150, in June 1974. The photograph was taken at Lawrence Hill on Thursday 2 September 1976. When finally retired at the end of July 1977 I think it was the last of the training fleet to carry this cream livery with orange trimmings. A new general manager had come from Eastern National and brought with him the blue and red scheme seen in the background.

With a cheery thumbs-up for the lorry driver who has 'flashed him out', the driver of FLF6G No. 7228 (EHT 117C) gets going in Church Road, St George. This particular bus stop was still requested by elderly residents of the area as 'the Park Picture House'. The establishment had been demolished in 1964. By Friday 2 May 1980 the 88 service had been extended to fill the void left by the Hanham local services, becoming a long route. The 'Lodekka' badges from the front grilles tended to 'walk' during the final years of the FLFs. As we can see here, they concealed the aperture for a starting handle.

In 1980 the company acquired an entire batch of VRTs from London Country Bus Services, for whom they were a non-standard element in a double-deck fleet composed of Leyland Atlanteans. These buses were unusual in that they were built to a height of 14 feet 5 inches. The depth of the side panels suggests that the gain was in lower deck headroom. They were powered by Leyland 0.501 engines, but the company soon began to replace these with Gardner LXBs. No. 6512 (PPH 473R) is seen at CRW on Saturday 20 December 1980. Many entered service in Bristol still carrying a complete complement of Grays and Tilbury area advertising.

The Gardner LW series of engines appeared in 1931 and remained in production, virtually unmodified, until 1974. Many bus operators 'swore by' these superbly engineered, almost indestructible engines. Tales of their longevity and durability were numerous. They were made in blocks of between one and four cylinders and could be assembled in any combination. In the 1950s a horizontal version was produced for use in underfloor-engined buses. Here, at CRW on Thursday 25 October 1979, we see a rack of three five-cylinder HLWs (H for Horizontal) and one (bottom right) six-cylinder version, probably salvaged from MW buses.

Since time immemorial dual-purpose buses had been numbered in the 20XX series and coaches in the 21XX. The former No. 2047 (KHW 316E) survived long enough to find itself renumbered into a new series of numbers introduced in April 1979. The seven-strong KHW-E batch had the same brakes as MWs, which were completely inadequate for the larger, heavier, faster and more powerful RE; it was essential to adapt your driving technique. On Friday 13 July 1979, No. 2442 (as it had become) gets away from the Guthrie Road entrance of Bristol Zoo with what appears to be a school party, presumably returning to Weston-super-Mare, where the vehicle was based.

In spite of appearances to the contrary, this Bristol-engined FLF Lodekka was Bristol's former No. C7162 (AHT 718B). Following withdrawal on the last day of 1977 it passed, through a dealer, to Mr Lift Fork Lift Trucks, which operated from premises off the A38 at Rudgeway. The owner of the business, a Mr Day, re-registered the bus as DAY 787. The photograph dates from Wednesday 24 January 1979.

The company's last pair of MWs saw out their final three months working from Trowbridge. No. 2590 (983 UHW) and its twin, No. 2589, were withdrawn on 31 October 1979. Both had been new in February 1964. With less than a fortnight to go, No. 2590 is seen at the town's modest bus station loading up for Devizes on Friday 19 October 1979.

Nailsea was an expanding town whose bus services were subject to much revision and extension. The 354 from Bristol, instead of operating to its terminus, turning around and returning the same way, now waited half way around a 'terminal loop'. I disliked this arrangement, which increased the likelihood of passengers remaining on the bus during the overlay. RELL No. 1033 (MAE 152F) is posed in Hannah More Road, Nailsea. The last passenger had just alighted, but up ahead, at the terminus, a little knot of old dears could be seen, holding their hot little handfuls of local authority concessionary fare tokens.

The earliest VRTs in the fleet were regulars on the 22/23 services. As the 2/2A, the service had once been provided from Eastville depot. When Eastville closed it was provided from Lawrence Hill and was combined into a single roster with the 10s. When driver-only operation came, the 22/23s went to Muller Road and the 10s to Winterstoke Road. No. 5003 (EHU 362K) was snapped on Wednesday 16 January 1980 in Romney Avenue, Lockleaze, on the brow of the descent from Purdown.

Training bus No. W154 (834 CHU) is seen on Friday 6 April 1979 against a venerable group of shopfronts, now vanished, in Old Market Street. The bus, new in 1958 as No. L8468, was withdrawn in October 1973, but was returned to service as a temporary training bus in January 1974. Temporary training buses were without internal modification and reserved for the more advanced trainees, often former lorry drivers pressured by their wives into seeking more regular work. The bus became a permanent trainer in August 1975, but was never modified.

The last Lodekka bought new by the company leaves Staple Hill depot to take up a school run on the afternoon of Wednesday 2 April 1980. It had entered service with a Bristol engine, but most FLFs likely to survive late had now been re-engined with Gardners. In the background two Leyland Nationals await departure on the 13 and 14 services. Staple Hill had been a tram depot. It closed not long after the photograph was taken, a few months after the company had asphalted the previously unsurfaced parking area at the side of the building.

The Leyland National 2 was a great change for the better, although much of the improvement dwelt in the extent to which the original vehicle's innovations had been dropped. The familiar roof 'pod' and its heating and ventilation equipment became an option, seldom exercised. The clanking, smoky Leyland 0.510 engine had gone, replaced by an updated version of the well-tried 0.680. Moquette upholstery returned after years of chill vinyl. There were no ribbed roof panels to direct blinding cataracts of rainwater down the windscreen when you braked. The wipers still tended to get stuck at the edges of the windscreen and the preposterous switch layout was perpetuated, but half a loaf is better than no bread. No. 3517 (AAE 661V) is seen climbing out of Bath on the Wells Road on Monday 15 September 1980.

The dual-purpose RELHs might have been regarded as bus-like coaches or coach-like buses, but in those with the 'BET' curved front, the bus seemed to achieve ascendancy over the coach. With a pair of fitters in charge, No. 2070 (GHY 132K) prepares to turn from Beach Road into Weston-super-Mare's vanished bus station. It had probably been out on a test drive after some remedial work.

An odd and decidedly non-standard purchase in 1980 was a batch of five MCW Metrobuses with Rolls-Royce Eagle engines. All received advertising liveries promoting the company's various bargain tickets and fare cards – in the case of No. 6002 (DAE 512W) the off-peak day return. The bus is seen at Lawrence Hill on Saturday 20 December 1980. All the Metrobuses went into service at Bath.

I think the 77/78 service was eventually converted to driver-only operation using Leyland Olympians, so this was probably a crewed VRT being used at a time when the service was still normally operated by FLFs. No. 5113 (RHT 507S) negotiates the customary obstacles in Gloucester Road, augmented on this occasion, Monday 15 May 1980, by road works and traffic cones. This location, Nevil Road when considered as a fare stage, was often requested by passengers as 'the top of Pigsty Hill' – a name that, rather like 'the Centre', has no formal existence and appears on no map.

An early 11.3-metre, dual-door Leyland National, No. 1404 (JHU 845L) is seen on Wednesday 16 January 1980 a few hundred yards from its home depot, Muller Road. By this time Nationals were the only single-deck type allocated there. The 89 was 'orbital' in nature, connecting the northern to the easterly suburbs. Here the route was shared for a short distance with the 22/23: the two bus stops were probably considered necessary because of the disorderly multitude that gathered here every afternoon from the nearby St Thomas More School.

One of the former Trowbridge FLF Lodekkas makes a rare appearance in Bristol on Good Friday, 4 April 1980. All but one were eventually transferred to Bath and might have been expected to appear regularly on the 339 service to Bristol, but seldom did. A feature of these buses was the extra luggage rack, seen at the front of the lower deck, reducing seating capacity to sixty-eight. The edifice in the background had been the company's head office, and one of the city's landmark buildings. The company vacated in 1969 but for a while crew relief facilities were retained. These were eventually moved elsewhere and at the time of the photo the structure was derelict. A bland re-modelling took place in the early eighties.

In July 1972 this dual-door RELL, No. 1275 (EHU 376K), was delivered with a Leyland 0.510 – the engine that was to be fitted to the Leyland National, then under development and about to go into production. Another RELL, No. C1129, which had the usual Leyland 0.680 unit, was re-engined with a 0.510 engine in April 1973. Both buses often worked from Hanham depot, whose main service, the 380, passed along the street in which I lived. Very early in the morning, when all around was still, the rise and fall of the turbocharger whistle, especially of No. C1129, could be heard literally from miles away. Some means must have been found of silencing this feature, which suddenly was heard no more.

When it entered service in February 1971 as coach No. 2157 (YHU 521J), this Leyland 'Leopard' PSU3A/4R was the first Leyland single-deck chassis and first Plaxton body to be ordered by the company. When, in line with the company's usual policy, these coaches were downgraded to dual-purpose, there was some opposition from the men's union to their use on stage-carriage bus work. The union was eventually appeased, but the vehicles were never accounted a great success in the bus role and were not used for long. By this time numbered into the dual-purpose series as 2085, the vehicle is seen in Beach Road, Weston-super-Mare, on Saturday 15 September 1979.

During the early eighties crew operation using FLF Lodekkas disappeared from the larger towns throughout the company's area and retreated to Bristol itself. The last such service at Weston-super-Mare was the 105 from Oldmixon Estate to Worle. No. 7257 (FHY 127D) passes neatly clipped privet in Milton Road on Friday 22 August 1980. It retains its full-depth front wings. These were often – but not always – cut back to improve cooling of the front brakes and because they were found to be vulnerable to damage in minor collisions.

The 51 service was the easterly end of the former 84, which had originated from a lonely lay-by among hedges and fields at Cribbs Causeway, long before the M5 motorway and today's vast shopping mall. On Thursday 11 September 1980, RELL No. 1231 (AHT 215J) noses out from the bus stop into the stationary traffic at the Lodge Causeway traffic lights in Fishponds Road. The point at which the traffic started to move was usually the moment when an intending passenger would tap on the door in the expectation of being let aboard. Sometimes it was necessary to harden one's heart.

VRT No. 5106 (PHY 700S) was new in November 1977 and, in May 1979, was repainted in an all-over advertising livery for Great Mills Warehouses. On Tuesday 15 January 1980 it was to be found operating from Muller Road depot on the 71 service and was photographed at Melvin Square, Knowle West. A week or two later it was loaned to Western National to give wider publicity to the client.

In exchange for the bus seen in the previous photo, Bristol received Western National's No. 1113 (VDV 113S), seen here in Bell Hill Road, St George, on Friday 2 May 1980. The 87 was still worked by crewed FLFs and the Western National vehicle was presumably excluded by its single door from working on driver-only routes within the city. Those who take photographs of buses become accustomed to funny looks from passengers.

The FLF type was becoming thin on the ground by the time of this photo, taken on Thursday 11 September 1980. Two or three services were still operated all day by these vehicles, but elsewhere there were only school and works journeys and peak-hour extras – known, in company lingo, for obscure reasons, as 'jazzers'. The 91 was an all-day service connecting Filton with the easterly suburbs of Kingswood and Hanham and augmented at peak hours by extra buses for aircraft workers. Bristol-engined No. 7206 (DHW 981C) turns from Fishponds Road into Lodge Causeway, where the road rises to cross the former Midland railway line.

'I'm afraid I shall have to report this.' The speaker produced a notebook, identified himself as a town councillor and referred me to the notice, prohibiting HGVs, at the entrance to Rock Street car park, Thornbury. The man didn't seem to understand that a bus is not an HGV, but also I was working a 'stop out' duty that kept me away from my home depot's canteen facilities all day. It was therefore 'union agreement' that it included a minimum of thirty-five minutes of 'non driving time'. The driver's instructions, in black and white on his duty card, were to wait in Rock Street car park to avoid causing an obstruction in the high street. The company must have cleared this with the council. There is no better feeling than to be 'reported' when you know you are rock-solid in the right. RELL No. 1048 (MHW 852F) is pictured in the car park on Saturday 27 September 1980.

By the time of this photograph, Friday 29 August 1980, most of the surviving FLFs were, or had become, Gardner-engined. A minority, such as No. 7300 (JHW 68E), retained their Bristol BVW engines. The troublesome Cave-Brown-Cave apparatus had been dropped late in the production life of the FLF and the familiar air intakes on either side of the destination screen are absent. The company's crew relief facilities had now moved out of the old pastel-coloured, mock-Tudor building in the distance to the Colston Centre, high above the pavement on the right.

During the late 1970s the company assessed many 'midibuses' and small conventional buses for use on the 'Windmill Hill Community Bus'. This catered to the hill-dwelling folk of an area inaccessible to full-sized buses by reason of its steep, narrow streets lined from end to end with parked cars. Various vehicles were borrowed for short periods from other National Bus Company subsidiaries, but in the end the company acquired No. 304 (RPH 105L), a thirty-five-seat Bristol LHS, from London Country Bus Services. It is seen in the yard of Lawrence Hill depot on Saturday 27 September 1980.

RELL No. 1192 (YHU 512J) seldom ventured onto the roads in revenue-earning service: it was permanently set aside for training. Drivers were taught on KSWs and LDs with 'crash' gearboxes. The RE was 10 feet longer, with considerable overhang beyond the axles, and had semi-automatic transmission. It was therefore considered necessary to set one aside to 'familiarise' newly qualified drivers. Semi-autos were vulnerable to damage caused by misuse and correct technique was a great fetish of the engineering department. Instructors were fond of relating that this bus had given years of trouble-free service when driven under their supervision, but developed gearbox problems as soon as it was pressed into service at a time of vehicle shortage.

Another late-surviving Bristol-engined FLF Lodekka, No. 7165 (AHY 981B) proceeds along Greystoke Avenue, Southmead, in low winter sunshine on Wednesday 16 January 1980. The Arnside Road shops, in the background, were the focal point of the Southmead estate, in the 1970s notable for many instances of 'trouble' on the buses that served it. Police escorts for the 'boozers' bus' – the 22.48 departure, just after closing time, from Broad Quay on the city centre – were not unknown.

A Bath stalwart all its life, RESL No. 520 (YHT 806J) stands in Newark Street, probably waiting for a driver to materialise from the bus station canteen. The extra 5 inches to the curved windscreens brought these short-wheelbase REs up to 32 feet 9 inches. The bus, new only in October 1970, was photographed on Monday 15 September 1980 and had probably not long to go. For many years the company's policy had been to favour large single-deckers but, suddenly, double-deckers were back in demand. Small single-deckers faced an insecure future.

There must have been a shortage of the usual dual-purpose RELHs on Tuesday 30 September 1980, for a humble RELL had been provided on the 09.00 departure from Bristol on the 301 limited stop service to Cardiff. No. 1051 (MHW 855F) had been among the buses temporarily re-allocated to Avonmouth depot in 1969, while the 'city' fleet awaited delivery of its own dual-door REs, to spearhead driver-only operation of the 15 service – the first of the city routes to be converted.

Although they were operating separate services from different depots, chance had thrown together two consecutively numbered FLFs at Filton on Saturday 17 May 1980. On the left, No. 7201 (CHY 419C) had been re-engined with a Gardner unit in 1973, whereas No. 7202 (CHY 420C) retained a Bristol engine. The 87 operated from Lawrence Hill, but No. 7202 was a 'traffic pool' bus, without a permanent allocation. Every depot had a unique destination blind and the blank display would suggest that another depot's blind had been left in place, making it impossible to show the correct destination.

Just across the road from the Blue Boy public house, VRT No. 5028 (MHW 295L) waits at Gainsborough Square, in artist-themed Lockleaze, to depart on the 23 for Shirehampton, far off on the opposite side of Bristol. The bus, photographed on Wednesday 16 January 1980, had led a slightly more eventful existence than most of its kindred, having spent three years as an all-over advertisement and been loaned for a month to City of Oxford Motor Services, working from its Bicester garage.

The 75 was, I believe, a new route introduced to provide a service to Little Stoke, whose previous country services had been discontinued under MAP. This kind of flexibility would not have been possible a few years earlier, when the city and country services were separate entities. With the coming of Bradley Stoke, Abbey Wood and Aztec West, and the further development of Bristol Parkway station, the Cribbs Causeway shopping centre and the University of the West of England all this region, conterminous with Bristol's suburbs but administratively in South Gloucestershire, was to see great upheavals. Re-engined FLF6G No. 7285 (JAE 94D) was pictured in Station Road, Filton, which has since been incorporated into the Avon Ring Road, on Tuesday 3 February 1981.

The good looks of this early coach-shell ECW body, with a Lodekka-style grille, had survived several switches from coach to dual-purpose livery since RELH No. 2079 (NHW 308F) had entered service as a Bristol Greyhound coach in April 1968. By Thursday 1 November 1979, when it was photographed entering Swindon bus station, it had recently been re-painted into the dual-purpose colour scheme in which it was to see out its last years.

Wet days tended to generate a high yield of 'short dappers', who caught the bus over distances they would have walked on a fine day. These passengers, alighting in Bristol's city centre from a well steamed-up No. 7226 (EHT 115C), had probably travelled the two stops from Queen's Road. There also would have probably been a high yield of left-behind umbrellas for the Lost Property Office. The photograph dates from Friday 29 August 1980. The bus had spent eleven years at Stroud, but been re-allocated to Hanham in September 1976. The Hanham 'linen', or destination blind, would not have included the correct destination for Lawrence Hill's 87 service.

New in 1974 and acquired by the company in 1977, No. W171 (GPH 663N) was a Ford D1311 7-ton stores lorry. It appears to be equipped with a crane manufactured by the Suedo-Finnish company Hydrauliska Industri AB. The other vehicle was probably No. W145, another stores lorry, this time a Leyland Boxer 1300BX/34R new in February 1973. The photograph was taken at CRW, Lawrence Hill, on Saturday 8 December 1979.

I think by Wednesday 10 May 1978, the 432 Bristol–Cirencester service had already been cut back to Tetbury. In any case this was a short working: the 06.09 journey from Bristol went only to Hawkesbury Upton. The location is Little Sodbury. In another few hundred yards the bus will start to climb through the village of Horton and soon after will find itself among broad wheat fields and dry-stone walls on the oolitic limestone of the Cotswolds. RELL No. 1051 (MHW 855F) makes a second appearance in our book.

Bristol LH6L No. 405 (REU 316S) was just a year old when photographed on Tuesday 23 January 1979. This duty worked out to Thornbury from Bristol, then proceeded to Sharpness via Rockhampton and Hill, and finally reached Dursley on the 414 service (which was numbered among the Stroud-area routes). It returned to Bristol the same way it had come. This was taken on the second time of calling at Sharpness, by which time the weather had taken a turn for the worse.

Considering that it was high summer – more precisely, Friday 22 August 1980 – it is surprising that convertible FS No. 8578 (868 NHT) was running with its roof fitted. It was during the 1980 season that these veterans of the Weston-super-Mare seafront service, new in 1961, began to give way to newer open-toppers acquired second-hand and converted by the company. The bus, seen in Milton Road, had gained this colour scheme at the beginning of the 1976 season.

FLF No. 7285 (JAE 94D) works its way into the traffic by sheer force of personality as Patchway's aircraft workers make their way home after a stint of Saturday morning double-time. It is lunchtime on Saturday 17 May 1980 and we are across the road from the offices of British Aerospace at Filton – although Bristolians had never got out of the habit of referring to 'B. A. C.'

Withdrawn well before their time by the Bristol company, several of the early RESLs were snapped up by National Welsh, who knew a bargain when they saw one. Powered by the 11.1-litre Leyland 0.680 engine, these small buses were no sluggards. National Welsh was a merger, under NBC auspices, of the former Western Welsh and Red & White companies. Many almost-new LH-types were also bought by other operators who seemed less persuaded than Bristol of the need to be rid of small buses. The former Bristol No. 503 (THU 349G), a veteran of Bath depot, is seen at Cardiff bus station on Tuesday 13 December 1980.

The company's first batch of six LHs was unusual in having semi-automatic transmission. Not popular with drivers, they were always allocated to Weston-super-Mare or Wells depots. Cream window-sealing rubber, twin headlights and indicators at the corners made them look rather RE-like from the front. It was some years before the company took any more LHs and all had manual gearboxes. No. 353 (DHW 293K) was snapped at the 'town' end of Locking Road, Weston-super-Mare, on Saturday 16 June 1979. It was withdrawn the following year, but served for a further seventeen years with Thomas of Llangadog, following which it was acquired for preservation.

Two-man 'crew' operation survived longest on the busiest routes. Thus, the 73/74, 77/78 and 87/88 became a kind of *salon de refusés* of the oldest vehicles in the fleet and of long-serving crews with contracts dating from before staff were required to sign an undertaking to train as driver-only operators. The 87/88 became, in July 1984, the last bus service in the country worked by the Bristol Lodekka. FLF-type No. 7170 (BHU 19C) is seen in Broad Weir on Wednesday 16 May 1979 against a background that entirely disappeared during the 1990s.

Swindon's No. 5522 (PEU 517R) picks up in Fleming Way on Wednesday 17 September 1980 carrying an all-over advertising livery for Anchor butter. Anchor were a big local employer. The bus was a standard, off-the-peg VRT with a Gardner LXB engine, of a type endemic throughout the NBC.

Let us end as we began, with a Bristol KSW. At the conclusion of the period covered by this book, on Friday 2 May 1980, beginners were still being taught the old way on training bus No. W143 (UHY 384), which had been new in 1955 as No. 8336. When withdrawn from the main fleet in November 1972, it had been the last of the 'country' fleet KSWs with platform doors and a five-speed gearbox. The trainee practices his skills in Bell Hill Road, St George. The 'Kingswood main road' was perennially clogged with parked cars over much of its uphill climb from the centre of the city.